COLLECTING
FIGURAL TAPE
MEASURES

WITH PRICE GUIDE

Elizabeth & Douglas Arbittier
and
Janet & John Morphy

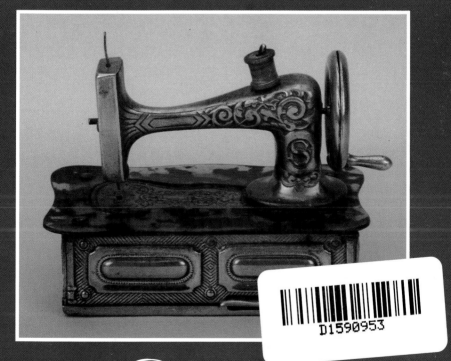

77 Lower Valley Road, Atglen, PA 19310

Dedication

To our parents, who gave us such tremendous support, and to our daughter Bonnie, our greatest asset. Also to Lu and Sid, the wonderful people who helped to develop our appreciation for antiques.
--E.J.A. and D.A.A.

With pride, to the four most important people in our lives: our sons, John and Dan, and our daughters, Heather and Amber. Thanks, kids, for being the great people that you are.
--J.M. and J.M.

Copyright © 1995 by Liz & Doug Arbittier and Janet & John Morphy.

Printed in China.
ISBN: 0-88740-866-4

Library of Congress Cataloging-in-Publication Data

Arbittier, Elizabeth.
    Collecting figural tape measures with price guide/Elizabeth & Douglas Arbittier and Janet & John Morphy.
        p.   cm.
    Includes bibliographical references.
    ISBN 0-88740-866-4
    1. Measuring-tapes--Collectors and collecting--Catalogs. I. Arbittier, Douglas. II. Morphy, Janet. III. Morphy, John. IV. Title.
NK6300.A73 1995
646'.19--dc20   95-24050
                                        CIP

Published by Schiffer Publishing, Ltd.
77 Lower Valley Road
Atglen, PA 19310

Please write for a free catalog.
This book may be purchased from the publisher.
Please include $2.95 for shipping.
Try your bookstore first.

We are interested in hearing from authors with book ideas on related subjects.

Description: Potted plant with berries
Material: Brass
Origin: Unknown
Mechanism: Wind-up
Height: 3"
Value Index: 5

Opposite photo: See page 86.

Contents

Acknowledgments

So many people have helped us with this book that this brief list is bound to exclude someone, and for this we apologize. Most importantly, we want to thank Louise Lippert, without whose help this book would surely not exist. The contribution of her tape measure collection for photographs, her time, and her knowledge were invaluable.

We also appreciate the help of all of the following: Lois Riggle, Lucille and Sidney Malitz, David and Deborah Sokol, Mildred Detrick, George Hattersley, Nancy Resnick, Matt Andres, Kim McCann, Bill and Susan Johnston, Daniel Shackman Jacoby, Joan Hahne, David Romano, Estelle Horowitz, Jolene Cooper, Marjorie Geddes, Lois Alterman, and Rosalind Berman.

If you have any questions or additional information, please contact the authors through Schiffer Publishing Ltd.

Description: Tapes from the 1940s and 1950s (selection)
Material: Ceramic, plastic
Origin: Unknown
Mechanism: Spring
Height: varies 2"-4"
Rarity: 1

Introduction

Antique sewing items have long been popular collectibles. There are many subspecialties in this collecting field, including samplers, darning eggs, thimbles, thimble cases, and needle cases. There are several good collecting guides written about these items as well as a number of general sewing collectible books, but none has thus far dealt in detail with the figural tape measure.

Far from being a simple means of measurement, tape measures were often an expression of creativity, artistry and/or humor. The last few years have seen an increased interest in these objects, and this book serves as an introduction to the figural type of sewing tape measure popular from about 1820 through the 1950s.

The earliest recorded measurements were used for primitive construction and have been recorded as far back as 8000 B.C. The standard measure at that time was the cubit, or the length of a man's forearm from fingertip to elbow. Obviously, this was a widely varied measurement. Sophistication of measurements increased through the centuries until King Henry I of England, in the twelfth century, required that the yard be equal to 36 inches, which was the length of his arm.

After the yard had been standardized, measuring sticks called meteyards were developed. They were the length of the standard yard. From these meteyards, seamstresses made cloth tape measures by measuring a length of ribbon along the stick's length. The ribbon was much easier to transport and, once it frayed, could be easily replaced with another ribbon measured from the original stick.

The older meteyards used letters rather than numbers to represent fractions of the yard. These letters were transferred to the cloth tape measures made from the measuring sticks. "Y" represented an entire yard; "HY" marked a half yard; "Q" was a quarter-yard; "HQ" was half a quarter-yard, or 4 1/2 inches; and "N" measured a nail, or 2 1/4 inches (figure 1). These markings were used into the early 19th century. As the inch became the standard, however, the nail and yard abbreviations were used less, until they were obsolete by the mid-19th century.

The earliest casings for cloth tape measures appear to have been small receptacles of valuable metals in the seventeenth century. Tapes were also wound into small shells. The earliest figural casings were produced in eighteenth

Figure 1.

century Europe. These early tapes varied in origin, and thus in their markings of measurement, until 1799 when the metric system was adopted throughout Europe. After that time, one side of the tape might have been marked in inches, the other side in centimeters. This practice became even more popular with greater exportation to America and England.

Figural tapes originated in several countries and varied in material. Usually, brass tapes dating from the late nineteenth/early twentieth centuries were made in Germany. Hardier celluloid tape measures from ca. 1920-30 were also from Germany. Most thinner celluloid casings were produced in Japan and date to ca. 1930-50. Porcelain tapes date to ca. 1920-30, and the majority were made in Germany. Other less common casing materials included bakelite, vegetable ivory, bronze, pewter, wood, nickel, plaster, and white metal.

The country of origin could be molded or stamped on the tape casing and/or printed on the tape itself (figure 2). A number of tapes are marked "LONDON Made in Austria." These are mostly enclosed in Vienna bronze or white metal casings and were likely made for export. Many of the German tapes were made for export as well, and appeared in American novelty catalogs (figure 3).

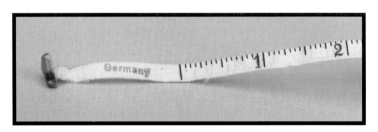

Figure 2.

FAVOR CANDLESTICKS AND CANDELABRA

		Per dozen	Ea.
1202	Silver Candelabra, three prongs, 3¼ inches...........	$1.10	$0.
1203	Silver Candelabra, five prongs, 3½ inches.............	1.70	
1204	Miniature "Old Fashioned Candlestick, "red, 2¼ inches	.85	

On above four kinds, the price includes one taper for each prong. Extra tapers can be purchased at 10c. per box (2 dozen in a box).

Novelty Tape Measures

These are well made novelties with tape measures concealed. Mal very unique favors.

1227	1228

		Per dozen	Eac
1225	Mandolin Tape Measure, celluloid, 3 inches...........	$3.90	$0.
1226	Stein Tape Measure, celluloid, 1¾ inches.............	2.80	
1227	Donkey Tape Measure. Brass metal, 2¾ inches........	5.50	
1228	Drum with Sticks Tape Measure. Brass metal, 2¾ ins.	5.50	
1229	Cash Register Tape Measure. Brass metal, 2¼ inches.	5.50	
1230	Tea Kettle Tape Measure. Brass metal, 2¾ inches.....	5.50	
1231	Automobile Tape Measure. Brass metal, 3 inches.....	5.50	
1232	Balloon Tape Measure. Brass metal, 2½ inches........	5.50	

1233	1234	1235

		Per dozen
1233	Alarm Clock Tape Measure. Brass metal, 2½ inches..	$5.50
1234	Tray with Bottle and Thimble Glass. Tape Measure. Silver metal, 3¼ inches......................	5.50
1235	Violin with Bow Tape Measure. Brass metal, 2¾ ins.	5.50

NOVELTY TAPE MEASURES—Continued

		Per dozen	Each
1236	Pig Tape Measure. Brass metal, 2¼ inches........	$2.90	$0.25
1237	Cat Tape Measure. Brass metal, 3 inches..........	5.50	.50
1238	Letter Press Tape Measure. Brass metal, 2¾ inches..	5.50	.50
1239	Market Basket Tape Measure. Brass metal, with movable rabbit, 2¾ inches............................	5.50	.50
1240	Round Owl Tape Measure. Brass metal, 1½ inches...	2.75	.25
1241	Round Cat Tape Measure. Brass metal, 1½ inches...	2.75	.25

1242	1243

		Per dozen	Each
1242	Green Frog Tape Measure. Celluloid, 2¾ inches......	$2.90	$0.25
1243	Turtle Tape Measure. Celluloid, 3½ inches..........	2.90	.25
1244	Apple Tape Measure. Celluloid, 1½ inches..........	2.80	.25
1245	Pear Tape Measure. Celluloid, 2 inches............	2.80	.25
1246	Orange Tape Measure. Celluloid, 1½ inches.........	2.80	.25
1247	Jockey Cap Tape Measure. Celluloid, 2 inches......	2.80	.25
1248	Duck Tape Measure. Celluloid, 2¾ inches..........	2.90	.25
1249	Fish Tape Measure. Celluloid, 4 inches............	2.90	.25
1250	Roly Poly Tape Measure. Celluloid, 2½ inches......	2.90	.25
1251	Black Cat's Head Tape Measure. Celluloid, 2 inches..	2.90	.25
1252	Red, White and Blue Celluloid Tape Measure, round, 1½ inches	2.90	.25

Novelty Match Safes (Brass Metal)

1260	1261

		Per dozen	Each
1260	Owl Match Safe. Brass metal, 2¼ inches..............	$5.50	$0.50
1261	Skull Head Match Safe. Brass metal, 2¼ inches......	5.50	.50
1262	Devil Head Match Safe. Brass metal, 2¼ inches......	5.90	.50
1263	Violin Match Safe. Brass metal, 2¾ inches..........	5.50	.50
1264	Rooster Head Match Safe. Brass metal, 2¼ inches...	5.50	.50

Fairy Table Lamps (Continued)

		Dozen	Ea.
1221	Rose Fairy Lamp, on foliage. American Beauty shape, lies flat on table, 5 inches	$6.90	$0.6
1222	Fairy Lamp, frosted	2.25	.
1223	Patent Candle Bulbs, burns 2 hours. 1 dozen in box. Not less than a box sold		.40

Novelty Tape Measures

		Dozen	Ea.
1230	Derby Hat, Tape Measure, 2¼ inches	$2.80	$0.2
1231	Hat Box, Tape Measure, 1½ inches	2.80	.2
1232	Panama Hat, Tape Measure, 2¼ inches	2.80	.2
1233	Purse, Tape Measure, 1½ inches	2.80	.2
1234	Barrel, Tape Measure 1½ inches	2.80	.2
1235	Acorn, Tape Measure, 2 inches	2.80	.2
1236	Clothes Iron, Tape Measure, 2½ inches	2.80	.2
1237	Watch, Tape Measure, 2 inches	2.80	.2
1238	Pig, Tape Measure, 3 inches	2.80	.2
1239	Wash Tub, with Mirror, Tape Measure, 1½ inches .	2.80	.2
1240	Horseshoe, Tape Measure, 1½ inches	2.80	.2
1241	Oranges, Tape Measure, 1¾ inches	2.80	.2
1242	Jug, Tape Measure, 1¾ inches	2.80	.2
1243	Sprinkling Can, Tape Measure 2 inches	2.80	.2
1244	Coffee Mill, Tape Measure, 2 inches	4.50	.4
1245	Mandolin, Tape Measure, 3 inches	4.50	.4
1246	Owl, with Hat, Tape Measure, 3½ inches	5.50	.5
1247	Parrot, Tape Measure 3½ inches	5.50	.5
1248	Bear, with stick, Tape Measure, 4 inches	5.50	.5
1249	Coon Banjo Player, Tape Measure, 4½ inches . . .	5.50	.5
1250	Lion, Tape Measure, 4 inches	5.50	.5
1251	Harp, Tape Measure, 4 inches	5.50	.5
1252	Basket, with 2 Puppies, Tape Measure, 3 inches . . .	5.50	.5
1253	Metal Automobile, Tape Measure, 2½ inches . . .	5.50	.5
1254	Diver, with Helmet, Tape Measure, 3½ inches . . .	3.90	.3
1255	Black Piano, Tape Measure, 1¾ inches	2.80	.2
1256	Camera, Tape Measure, 1¾ inches	2.80	.2
1257	Lemons, Tape Measure, 1¾ inches	2.80	.2
1258	Apples, Tape Measure, 1¾ inches	2.80	.2

Small Novelties

		Dozen Pair	Pair
1260	Real Rubber Boots, 1 pair in box, 3 inches	$3.30	$0.30
1261	Real Storm Rubbers, 3¼ inches, 1 pair in box	3.90	.35

		Dozen	Each
1262	Celluloid and Silk Fan, with tassel, 4 inches	$2.90	$0.25
1263	Metal Thermometer, flower trimmings, 2¾ inches . . .	1.70	.15
1264	Metal Picture Frame, flower trimmings, 3 inches . . .	1.70	.15
1265	Leather Football, silk ribbon, 3 inches	1.70	.15
1266	Leather Boxing Gloves, 3 inches	1.70	.15
1267	Hot Water Bag, "for cold feet," 3¼ inches	1.10	.10

		Dozen	Each
1268	Miniature Toilet Set. Silk bag, with Comb, Mirror and Powder Puff, 2½ inches	$2.80	$0.25
1269	Round Music Box. Plays. 2 inches		--

Figure 3.

Some of the earliest tapes were encased in shells with delicate wind-up mechanisms (figure 4: See page 157). The wind-up tapes were standard until the 1860s, when springs were introduced, but they persisted into the twentieth century. Animal tails, worms in beaks, and car steering wheels are a few of the many creative examples of winding mechanisms. Equally interesting are the unusual tape ends, such as flies and ladybugs, found on some spring tapes. In the 1870s, the mechanism of the spring was combined with a button. The tape would stay out of the casing until the button was pressed.

Most tape measures only served the one purpose of being a measure. Some, however, served also as thimble holders, pincushions, or needle holders. Some held wax for waxing thread. Several of these accessories were sometimes combined with the measure for an all-in-one sewing tool (figure 5).

Figure 5.

Some figural tape measures were made in series, having matching bases, identical tape ends, or common themes. Figures 6-8 show some of these in a variety of materials.

Figure 6.

Figure 7.

Figure 8.

Because of the broad range of tape measure prices, we propose a Value Index system for rating the tapes. Prices associated with this rating scale are listed below. While increase in rarity generally corresponds to increase in value, this does not always hold true. For example, some unusual celluloid tape measures may be valued less than a more common metal wind-up tape. All prices are retail and reflect tape measures in excellent condition. Also, prices vary considerably in different parts of the country. While prices have increased considerably in the last few years, bargains still can be found in flea markets and house sales.

Value Index System

Value 1:	$ 20- 60		Value 4:	$200-250
Value 2:	$ 60-120		Value 5:	$250-300
Value 3:	$120-200		Value R:	Over $300

Chapter 1
Human figures

Figural tape measures portray humans in great variety. The full figures include males and females of all ages. Many types of dress highlight different nationalities, occupations, and time periods. Activities range from sledding to playing instruments to simply striking a formal pose.

The human heads reveal a rich variety of expression. Most are comical, although emotions range from deep thought to surprise. Several tape measures, especially those made of porcelain and celluloid, are portraits representing people famous during the time of manufacture.

Description: Man holding geese
Material: Brass
Origin: Unknown
Mechanism: Wind-up
Height: 3.25"
Value Index: 4

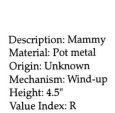

Description: Victorian lady on stand
Material: Brass
Origin: Unknown
Mechanism: Wind-up
Height: 2"
Value Index: 4

Description: Mammy
Material: Pot metal
Origin: Unknown
Mechanism: Wind-up
Height: 4.5"
Value Index: R

Description: English bobby on stand
Material: Brass
Origin: Unknown
Mechanism: Wind-up
Height: 2.5"
Value Index: 4

Description: Children on seesaw
Material: Brass
Origin: Unknown
Mechanism: Wind-up
Height: 2.25"
Value Index: 4

Description: Tailor on thimble
Material: Brass
Origin: Unknown
Mechanism: Wind-up
Height: 2"
Value Index: 4

Description: Girl in bonnet holding flowers
Material: Brass, celluloid
Origin: Unknown
Mechanism: Wind-up
Height: 2.5"
Value Index: 4

Description: Billiken
Material: Brass
Origin: Unknown
Mechanism: Wind-up
Height: 2.5"
Value Index: 4

Description: Noble lady
Material: White metal
Origin: Unknown

Mechanism: Spring
Height: 2.25"
Value Index: 4

Description: Jester (Punch)
Material: Brass
Origin: Unknown
Mechanism: Wind-up
Height: 2.5"
Value Index: 5

Left
Description: Bavarian boy on
    pedestal
Material: White metal
Origin: Unknown
Mechanism: Spring
Height: 2"
Value Index: 4

Right
Description: Bavarian girl on
    pedestal
Material: White metal
Origin: Unknown
Mechanism: Spring
Height: 2"
Value Index: 4

Description: "Aladdin" figure with lamp on
    patterned carpet
Material: Brass
Origin: Unknown
Mechanism: Spring
Height: 2"
Value Index: 5

Description: Indian with drum
Material: Lead
Origin: Germany
Mechanism: Spring
Height: 3.25"
Value Index: 5

Description: Black man on knees
Material: White metal
Origin: Unknown
Mechanism: Spring
Height: 1.75"
Value Index: 4

Left
Description: Black man with accordion
Material: Celluloid
Origin: Unknown
Mechanism: Spring
Height: 2"
Value Index: 4

Right
Description: Black man with banjo
Material: Celluloid
Origin: Germany
Mechanism: Spring
Height: 2"
Value Index: 4

14

Description: Black girl with apple
Material: Celluloid
Origin: Unknown
Mechanism: Spring
Height: 2"
Value Index: 3

Description: Black figure on barrel
Material: Celluloid
Origin: Unknown
Mechanism: Spring
Height: 2"
Value Index: 3

Description: Black figure on block
Material: Celluloid
Origin: Unknown
Mechanism: Spring
Height: 1.75"
Value Index: 3

Description: Black dancer on stage
Material: Celluloid
Origin: Unknown
Mechanism: Spring
Height: 4"
Value Index: 5

Description: Figure dressed in red on barrel
Material: Celluloid
Origin: Unknown
Mechanism: Spring
Height: 1.75"
Value Index: 3

Description: Lady dressed in cape holding bouquet
Material: Celluloid
Origin: Unknown
Mechanism: Spring
Height: 3.25"
Value Index: 3

Description: Oriental man on base
Material: Celluloid
Origin: Unknown
Mechanism: Spring
Height: 1.25"
Value Index: 3

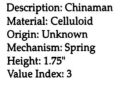

Description: Chinaman
Material: Celluloid
Origin: Unknown
Mechanism: Spring
Height: 1.75"
Value Index: 3

Description: Lady playing tambourine
Material: Celluloid
Origin: Unknown
Mechanism: Spring
Height: 3"
Value Index: 3

Description: Musketeer holding a pipe
Material: Celluloid
Origin: Unknown
Mechanism: Spring
Height: 3.5"
Value Index: 3

Description: Japanese man sitting with fan
Material: Celluloid
Origin: Unknown
Mechanism: Spring
Height: 2.25"
Value Index: 3

Description: Oriental man, carving a head
Material: Celluloid
Origin: Unknown
Mechanism: Spring
Height: 3.25"
Value Index: 3

Description: William Tell with son
Material: Celluloid
Origin: Unknown
Mechanism: Spring
Height: 3.5"
Value Index: 3

Description: Colonial man on base
Material: Celluloid
Origin: Unknown
Mechanism: Spring
Height: 2.5"
Value Index: 3

Description: Sailor with cannon, "THE HANDY
MAN"
Material: Celluloid
Origin: Unknown
Mechanism: Spring
Height: 3"
Value Index: 3

Description: Dutch boy on
pedestal
Material: Celluloid
Origin: Unknown
Mechanism: Spring
Height: 3.5"
Value Index: 4

Left
Description: Gentleman in tri-
cornered hat
Material: Celluloid
Origin: Germany
Mechanism: Spring
Height: 3.5"
Value Index: 3

Right
Description: Gentleman in tri-
cornered hat
Material: Celluloid
Origin: Germany
Mechanism: Spring
Height: 2.5"
Value Index: 3

19

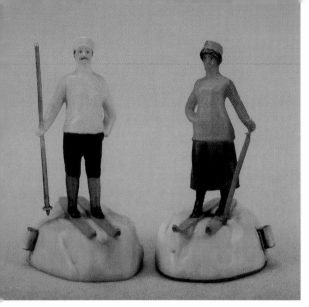

Left
Description: Male skier on rock
Material: Celluloid
Origin: Unknown
Mechanism: Spring
Height: 3"
Value Index: 4

Right
Description: Female skier on rock
Material: Celluloid
Origin: Unknown
Mechanism: Spring
Height: 3"
Value Index: 4

Left
Description: Dutch boy on pedestal
Material: Celluloid
Origin: Unknown
Mechanism: Spring
Height: 3.25"
Value Index: 4

Right
Description: Dutch girl on pedestal
Material: Celluloid
Origin: Unknown
Mechanism: Spring
Height: 3"
Value Index: 4

Description: Bobby on pedestal
Material: Celluloid
Origin: Unknown
Mechanism: Spring
Height: 3.5"
Value Index: 4

Description: Dutch boy on base
Material: Celluloid
Origin: Germany
Mechanism: Spring
Height: 2.5"
Value Index: 3

Description: Hoffbrau Beer emblem (friar in
  peaked cap and robe decorated with cross,
  holding beer stein)
Material: Celluloid
Origin: Unknown
Mechanism: Spring
Height: 3.5"
Value Index: 4

Left
Description: Male golfer on base
Material: Celluloid
Origin: Germany
Mechanism: Spring
Height: 3.25"
Value Index: 4

Right
Description: Dutch boy on pedestal
Material: Celluloid
Origin: Unknown
Mechanism: Spring
Height: 3"
Value Index: 4

Left
Description: Boy with bread box
Material: Celluloid
Origin: Germany
Mechanism: Spring
Height: 2.25"
Value Index: 4

Right
Description: Boy with basket of fish
Material: Celluloid
Origin: Japan
Mechanism: Spring
Height: 2"
Value Index: 4

Description: Rider on horse
Material: Celluloid
Origin: Unknown
Mechanism: Spring
Height: 2.5"
Value Index: 4

Description: Man riding camel
Material: Celluloid
Origin: Unknown
Mechanism: Spring
Height: 2.5"
Value Index: 4

Description: Indian on stump
Material: Celluloid
Origin: Japan
Mechanism: Spring
Height: 3"
Value Index: 3

Left
Description: Turbaned man on stepped base
Material: Celluloid
Origin: Germany
Mechanism: Spring
Height: 2"
Value Index: 3

Right
Description: Buddha on stepped base
Material: Celluloid
Origin: Germany
Mechanism: Spring
Height: 1.5"
Value Index: 3

Above left
Description: Seated man from India
Material: Celluloid
Origin: Unknown
Mechanism: Spring
Height: 1.75"
Value Index: 3

Above right
Description: Seated apple seller
Material: Celluloid
Origin: Unknown
Mechanism: Spring
Height: 1.75"
Value Index: 3

Description: Japanese woman with fan
Material: Celluloid
Origin: Unknown
Mechanism: Spring
Height: 2"
Value Index: 4

Description: Seated buddha
Material: Stippled celluloid
Origin: Unknown
Mechanism: Spring
Height: 1.75"
Value Index: 3

Description: Harlequin with mandolin and dog
Material: Celluloid
Origin: Unknown
Mechanism: Spring
Height: 2.25"
Value Index: 4

Left
Description: Lucky Joy Germ
Material: Celluloid
Origin: Japan
Mechanism: Spring
Height: 2"
Value Index: 3

Center
Description: Buddha, "GETTING BETTER AND BETTER DAY BY DAY IN EVERY WAY"
Material: Celluloid
Origin: Unknown
Mechanism: Spring
Height: 2"
Value Index: 3

Right
Description: Billiken
Material: Celluloid
Origin: Japan
Mechanism: Spring
Height: 2.5"
Value Index: 3

24

Left
Description: Colonial woman in full skirt, one
    leg showing
Material: Celluloid
Origin: Unknown
Mechanism: Spring
Height: 2.5"
Value Index: 3

Description: Colonial woman
    reading book
Material: Celluloid
Origin: Germany
Mechanism: Spring
Height: 2"
Value Index: 3

Right
Description: Victorian lady with full skirt
Material: Celluloid
Origin: Unknown
Mechanism: Spring
Height: 2.5"
Value Index: 3

Left
Description: Girl with flower baskets
Material: Celluloid
Origin: Unknown
Mechanism: Spring
Height: 2"
Value Index: 3

Right
Description: Boy with fruit baskets
Material: Celluloid
Origin: Germany
Mechanism: Spring
Height: 2.25"
Value Index: 3

Description: Swashbuckler
Material: Celluloid
Origin: Germany
Mechanism: Spring
Height: 2"
Value Index: 3

Left
Description: Girl with urn and fruit basket
Material: Celluloid
Origin: Unknown
Mechanism: Spring
Height: 1.75"
Value Index: 3

Right
Description: Girl with flowers, jumping dog
Material: Celluloid
Origin: Japan, Occupied Japan
Mechanism: Spring
Height: 2"
Value Index: 2

Description: Girl and boy sitting in flower basket
Material: Celluloid
Origin: Japan
Mechanism: Spring
Height: 2"
Value Index: 4

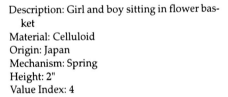

Description: Black Mammy
Material: Celluloid
Origin: Japan
Mechanism: Spring
Height: 2"
Value Index: 3

Left
Description: Sea captain with life
    preserver
Material: Celluloid
Origin: Unknown
Mechanism: Spring
Height: 2"
Value Index: 3

Right
Description: Dutch woman with
    basket
Material: Celluloid
Origin: Unknown
Mechanism: Spring
Height: 2"
Value Index: 3

Description: Woman sitting in beach cabana
Material: Celluloid
Origin: Unknown
Mechanism: Spring
Height: 2"
Value Index: 4

Description: Boy on sled
Material: Celluloid
Origin: Germany
Mechanism: Spring
Height: 2.25"
Value Index: 4

Description: Woman in straw chair
Material: Celluloid
Origin: Unknown
Mechanism: Spring
Height: 2"
Value Index: 3

27

Left
Description: Woman lounging in stuffed chair
Material: Celluloid
Origin: Unknown
Mechanism: Spring
Height: 1.75"
Value Index: 3

Right
Description: Woman playing mandolin
Material: Celluloid
Origin: Germany
Mechanism: Spring
Height: 2"
Value Index: 4

Description: Indian with bag of silver
Material: Celluloid
Origin: Unknown
Mechanism: Spring
Height: 2"
Value Index: 4

Left
Description: German man
Material: Celluloid
Origin: Germany
Mechanism: Spring
Height: 2.25"
Value Index: 3

Right
Description: German woman
Material: Celluloid
Origin: Germany
Mechanism: Spring
Height: 2.25"
Value Index: 3

Description: Indian boy in headdress (two color
varieties)
Material: Celluloid
Origin: Japan
Mechanism: Spring
Height: 2.5"
Value Index: 2

Description: Baseball player (two color variet-
ies)
Material: Celluloid
Origin: Japan
Mechanism: Spring
Height: 2"
Value Index: 3

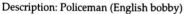

Description: Policeman (English bobby)
Material: Celluloid
Origin: Japan
Mechanism: Spring
Height: 2.5"
Value Index: 3

Description: Girl with muff and purse
Material: Celluloid
Origin: Germany
Mechanism: Spring
Height: 2"
Value Index: 3

Description: Girl with muff
Material: Celluloid
Origin: Unknown
Mechanism: Spring
Height: 2"
Value Index: 3

Description: Chef
Material: Celluloid
Origin: Germany
Mechanism: Spring
Height: 2"
Value Index: 4
Courtesy of Mildred Detrick

Description: Car driver
Material: Celluloid
Origin: Germany
Mechanism: Spring
Height: 3.5"
Value Index: 4
Courtesy of Mildred Detrick

Description: Golfer
Material: Celluloid
Origin: Germany
Mechanism: Spring
Height: 2"
Value Index: 4

Description: Sleeping Mexican
Material: Celluloid
Origin: Unknown
Mechanism: Spring
Height: 2"
Value Index: 3

Description: Clown on base
Material: Celluloid
Origin: Unknown
Mechanism: Spring
Height: 2.5"
Value Index: 3

Description: Indian boy on base
Material: Celluloid
Origin: Japan
Mechanism: Spring
Height: 2.75"
Value Index: 2

Description: Clown on base
Material: Celluloid
Origin: Germany
Mechanism: Spring
Height: 4"
Value Index: 3

31

Description: Young girl with finger in mouth
    (also needle case)
Material: Celluloid
Origin: Germany
Mechanism: Spring
Height: 2.75"
Value Index: 3

Description: Cowboy (two color variations)
Material: Celluloid
Origin: Japan
Mechanism: Spring
Height: 2.75"
Value Index: 2

Left
Description: Woman in white
    clingy skirt
Material: Celluloid
Origin: Occupied Japan
Mechanism: Spring
Height: 3"
Value Index: 3

Right
Description: Woman in white
    clingy skirt
Material: Celluloid
Origin: Occupied Japan
Mechanism: Spring
Height: 3"
Value Index: 3

Left
Description: Boy with thimble hat (also pincushion)
Material: Porcelain
Origin: Germany
Mechanism: Spring
Height: 4"
Value Index: 4

Right
Description: Girl with thimble hat (also pincushion)
Material: Porcelain
Origin: Germany
Mechanism: Spring
Height: 4"
Value Index: 4

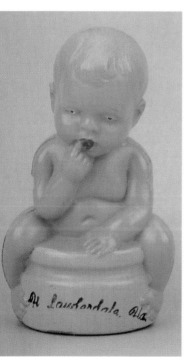

Description: Baby on potty
Material: Celluloid
Origin: Japan
Mechanism: Spring
Height: 2.75"
Value Index: 2

Left
Description: Man playing
mandolin, standing
Material: Porcelain
Origin: Germany
Mechanism: Spring
Height: 3.75"
Value Index: 4

Right
Description: Colonial lady
Material: Porcelain
Origin: Germany
Mechanism: Spring
Height: 4"
Value Index: 4

Opposite page, top left
Description: Bride
Material: Porcelain
Origin: Germany
Mechanism: Spring
Height: 4"
Value Index: 4

Right
Description: Groom
Material: Porcelain
Origin: Germany
Mechanism: Spring
Height: 4"
Value Index: 4

Left, right
Description: Dutch boy (two color variations)
Material: Porcelain
Origin: Germany
Mechanism: Spring
Height: 4"
Value Index: 3

Center
Description: Dutch girl
Material: Porcelain
Origin: Germany
Mechanism: Spring
Height: 4"
Value Index: 3

Description: Dancing girl
Material: Porcelain
Origin: Germany
Mechanism: Spring
Height: 4"
Value Index: 3

Left
Description: Dutch girl
Material: Porcelain
Origin: Unknown
Mechanism: Spring
Height: 3.5"
Value Index: 3

Right
Description: Dutch boy
Material: Porcelain
Origin: Unknown
Mechanism: Spring
Height: 3.5"
Value Index: 3

34

Description: German boy
Material: Porcelain
Origin: Germany
Mechanism: Spring
Height: 4"
Value Index: 3

Description: Girl playing mandolin, seated
Material: Porcelain
Origin: Germany
Mechanism: Spring
Height: 2.25"
Value Index: 3

Description: Dancing girl with sashed dress
Material: Porcelain
Origin: Germany
Mechanism: Spring
Height: 4"
Value Index: 3

Description: Man with flowers
Material: Porcelain
Origin: Germany
Mechanism: Spring
Height: 4"
Value Index: 4

Description: Ballerina (old style)
Material: Porcelain
Origin: Germany
Mechanism: Spring
Height: 4"
Value Index: 3

Left
Description: Seated lady
        with flowers
Material: Porcelain
Origin: Germany
Mechanism: Spring
Height: 2.25"
Value Index: 3

Right
Description: Seated lady
        with flowers
Material: Porcelain
Origin: Germany
Mechanism: Spring
Height: 2"
Value Index: 3

Description: Boy in riding habit
Material: Porcelain
Origin: Germany
Mechanism: Spring
Height: 3"
Value Index: 4

Description: Seated lady holding flower basket in front
Material: Porcelain
Origin: Germany
Mechanism: Spring
Height: 2.25"
Value Index: 3

Description: Girl clown
Material: Porcelain
Origin: Germany
Mechanism: Spring
Height: 3"
Value Index: 4
Courtesy of Mildred Detrick

Description: Child pierrot
Material: Porcelain
Origin: Germany
Mechanism: Spring
Height: 3.25"
Value Index: 4

Description: Girl from Norway
Material: Porcelain
Origin: Germany
Mechanism: Spring
Height: 3.5"
Value Index: 4

37

Description: Woman in gown holding rose
Material: Porcelain
Origin: Germany
Mechanism: Spring
Height: 3.5"
Value Index: 4
Courtesy of Mildred Detrick

Below
Description: Woman seated
   on basket of flowers (two
   color variations)
Material: Porcelain
Origin: Germany
Mechanism: Spring
Height: 3.75"
Value Index: 3

Description: Small harlequin
Material: Porcelain
Origin: Germany
Mechanism: Spring
Height: 2"
Value Index: 3

Description: Girl kneeling
Material: Porcelain
Origin: Germany
Mechanism: Spring
Height: 2.75"
Value Index: 4

Description: Man of India
Material: Porcelain
Origin: Germany
Mechanism: Spring
Height: 3.25"
Value Index: 4

Description: Boy clown
   holding mandolin
Material: Porcelain
Origin: Germany
Mechanism: Spring
Height: 4"
Value Index: 4

Description: Man squatting
Material: Porcelain
Origin: Germany
Mechanism: Spring
Height: 2.5"
Value Index: 3

Description: Dutch girl
Material: Porcelain
Origin: Germany
Mechanism: Spring
Height: 4"
Value Index: 3

Description: Old woman in chair
Material: Porcelain
Origin: Unknown
Mechanism: Spring
Height: 3"
Value Index: 4

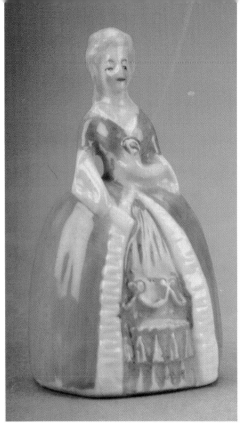

Description: French noble lady
Material: Porcelain
Origin: Unknown
Mechanism: Spring
Height: 3"
Value Index: 4

Description: Colonial man in long coat
Material: Porcelain
Origin: Unknown
Mechanism: Spring
Height: 5"
Value Index: 4

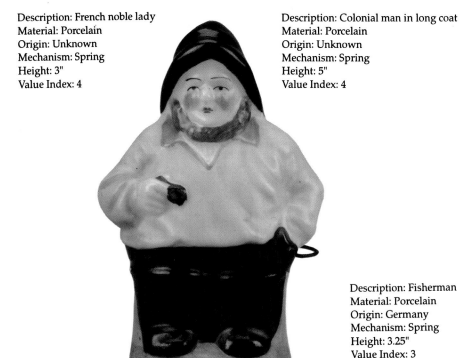

Description: Fisherman
Material: Porcelain
Origin: Germany
Mechanism: Spring
Height: 3.25"
Value Index: 3

Above left
Description: Woman in full skirt decorated with rose, holding fan
Material: Porcelain
Origin: Germany
Mechanism: Spring
Height: 2.5"
Value Index: 3

Above center
Description: Girl in striped dress
Material: Porcelain
Origin: Germany
Mechanism: Spring
Height: 3"
Value Index: 3

Above right:
Description: Woman in full skirt with sun hat
Material: Porcelain
Origin: Germany
Mechanism: Spring
Height: 3"
Value Index: 3

Description: Woman in full skirt with muff
Material: Porcelain
Origin: Unknown
Mechanism: Spring
Height: 2.75"
Value Index: 3

Description: Woman in green gown with small rose
Material: Porcelain
Origin: Germany
Mechanism: Spring
Height: 3.25"
Value Index: 4

41

Left
Description: Woman in flower petal skirt, scooped neckline
Material: Porcelain
Origin: Germany
Mechanism: Spring
Height: 3"
Value Index: 3

Right
Description: Woman in flower petal skirt, square neckline
Material: Porcelain
Origin: Germany
Mechanism: Spring
Height: 2.75"
Value Index: 3

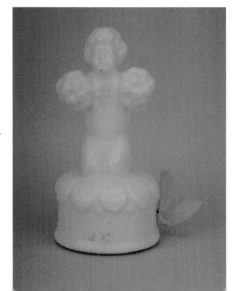

Description: Liberty of London (holds thimbles and needles)
Material: Cloth
Origin: Unknown
Mechanism: Spring
Height: 3.5"
Value Index: 1

Description: Kneeling girl on cushion (monochrome)
Material: Porcelain
Origin: Germany
Mechanism: Spring
Height: 3.25"
Value Index: 4

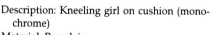

Description: Clown on stool (two color varia-
tions)
Material: Porcelain
Origin: Germany
Mechanism: Spring
Height: 3.75"
Value Index: 3

Description: Half dolls with crocheted skirts
(three varieties)
Material: Porcelain
Origin: Germany
Mechanism: Spring
Height: 3"
Value Index: 3

Description: Japanese woman
(pincushion)
Material: Plastic, cloth
Origin: Japan
Mechanism: Spring
Height: 3.5"
Value Index: 2

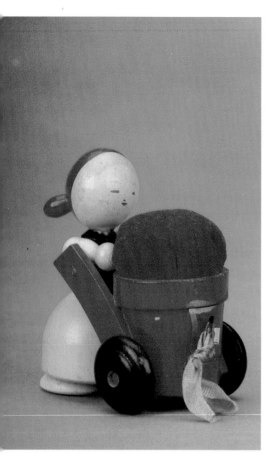

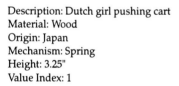

Description: Dutch girl pushing cart
Material: Wood
Origin: Japan
Mechanism: Spring
Height: 3.25"
Value Index: 1

Description: Indian woman
Material: Cloth, clay
Origin: Japan
Mechanism: Spring
Height: 3"
Value Index: 1

Chapter 2
Human heads

Left
Description: Devil
Material: White metal
Origin: Unknown
Mechanism: Wind-up
Height: 1.5"
Value Index: 5

Right
Description: Unknown man
Material: White metal
Origin: Unknown
Mechanism: Wind-up
Height: 2"
Value Index: 5

Description: Ubangi woman
  (hair is pincushion)
Material: White metal, felt
Origin: Unknown
Mechanism: Wind-up
Height: 2.5"
Value Index: R

Description: Clown with hat
Material: Celluloid
Origin: Unknown
Mechanism: Spring
Height: 2"
Value Index: 3

Description: Jester (two color variations)
Material: Celluloid
Origin: Germany
Mechanism: Spring
Height: 2"
Value Index: 2

Description: Clown
Material: Plastic
Origin: English
Mechanism: Wind-up
Height: 2.75"
Value Index: 2

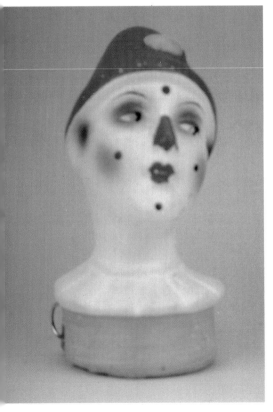

Description: Clown
Material: Clay
Origin: Unknown
Mechanism: Spring
Height: 3"
Value Index: 5

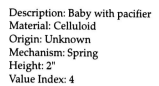
Description: Baby with pacifier
Material: Celluloid
Origin: Unknown
Mechanism: Spring
Height: 2"
Value Index: 4

Description: Baby crying, fly on forehead
Material: Celluloid
Origin: Unknown
Mechanism: Spring
Height: 2"
Value Index: 4

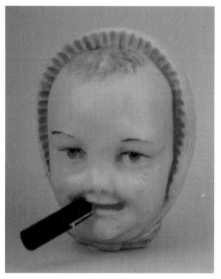

Description: Indian with cigar
Material: Celluloid
Origin: Unknown
Mechanism: Spring
Height: 2"
Value Index: 3

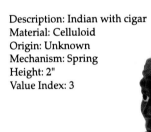

Description: Black man with cigarette
Material: Celluloid
Origin: Germany
Mechanism: Spring
Height: 1.5"
Value Index: 3

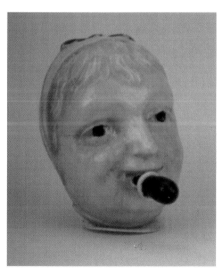

Description: Baby with pacifier
Material: Celluloid
Origin: Germany
Mechanism: Spring
Height: 1.75"
Value Index: 3

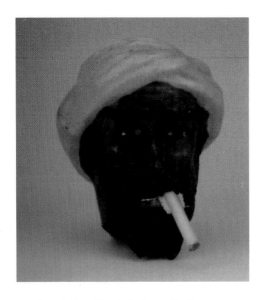

Description: Black man
Material: Celluloid
Origin: Unknown
Mechanism: Spring
Height: 2"
Value Index: 3

Description: Man in turban with cigarette
Material: Celluloid
Origin: Germany
Mechanism: Spring
Height: 1.75"
Value Index: 4

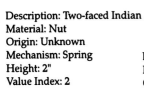

Description: Flapper with cigarette
Material: Celluloid
Origin: Germany
Mechanism: Spring
Height: 1.5"
Value Index: 3

Description: Two-faced Indian
Material: Nut
Origin: Unknown
Mechanism: Spring
Height: 2"
Value Index: 2

Description: Black girl
Material: Celluloid
Origin: Unknown
Mechanism: Spring
Height: 1.75"
Value Index: 3

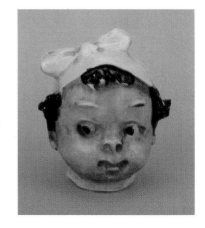

Description: Black boy
Material: Metal
Origin: Unknown
Mechanism: Wind-up
Height: 2.25"
Value Index: 3

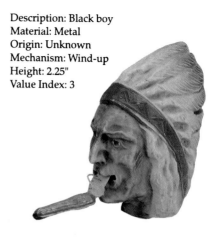

Description: Indian with full headdress
Material: Celluloid
Origin: Unknown
Mechanism: Spring
Height: 1.5"
Value Index: 3

Below left
Description: Indian boy with headdress
Material: Celluloid
Origin: Japan
Mechanism: Spring
Height: 2"
Value Index: 2

Below right
Description: Indian boy with two feathers
Material: Celluloid
Origin: Japan
Mechanism: Spring
Height: 2"
Value Index: 2

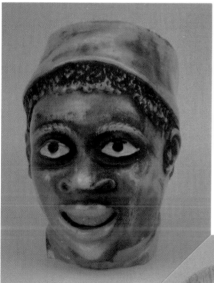

Description: Black man with fez
Material: Celluloid
Origin: Unknown
Mechanism: Spring
Height: 2.5"
Value Index: 4

Description: Man with monocle (Prime Minister Chamberlain)
Material: Celluloid
Origin: Unknown
Mechanism: Spring
Height: 2"
Value Index: 4

Description: Girl's head in bonnet
Material: Celluloid
Origin: Germany
Mechanism: Spring
Height: 1.75"
Value Index: 3

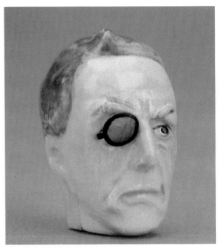

Description: Lady in green dress
Material: Celluloid
Origin: Unknown
Mechanism: Spring
Height: 2"
Value Index: 5

Description: Sailor with pipe (two color variations)
Material: Celluloid
Origin: Unknown
Mechanism: Spring
Height: 2"
Value Index: 4

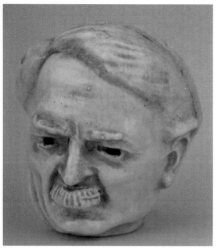

Description: Mark Twain (?)
Material: Celluloid
Origin: Unknown
Mechanism: Spring
Height: 2"
Value Index: 5

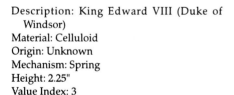

Description: Man with pipe (Stanley Baldwin?)
Material: Celluloid
Origin: Unknown
Mechanism: Spring
Height: 2"
Value Index: 4

Description: King Edward VIII (Duke of
    Windsor)
Material: Celluloid
Origin: Unknown
Mechanism: Spring
Height: 2.25"
Value Index: 3

Description: Man with cigar (Winston
    Churchill?)
Material: Celluloid
Origin: Unknown
Mechanism: Spring
Height: 2"
Value Index: 5

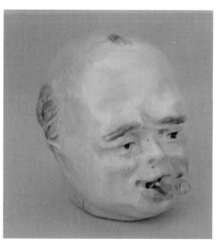

Description: Pilgrim (pincushion)
Material: Plastic
Origin: Japan
Mechanism: Spring
Height: 3.25"
Value Index: 3

Description: Napoleon
Material: Celluloid
Origin: Unknown
Mechanism: Spring
Height: 2.75"
Value Index: 4

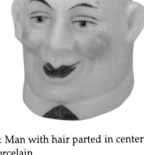

Description: Man with hair parted in center
Material: Porcelain
Origin: Germany
Mechanism: Spring
Height: 2"
Value Index: 4

Description: Lady half doll
Material: Porcelain
Origin: Germany
Mechanism: Spring
Height: 2.5"
Value Index: 4

Left	Center	Right
Description: Bald man with fly on head	Description: Bald man with fly on head	Description: Bald man with fly on head
Material: Porcelain	Material: Porcelain	Material: Porcelain
Origin: Germany	Origin: Germany	Origin: Germany
Mechanism: Spring	Mechanism: Spring	Mechanism: Spring
Height: 2"	Height: 1.75"	Height: 2"
Value Index: 4	Value Index: 4	Value Index: 4

Left	Center	Right
Description: Pierrot	Description: Pierrot	Description: Pierrot
Material: Porcelain	Material: Porcelain	Material: Porcelain
Origin: Germany	Origin: Germany	Origin: Germany
Mechanism: Spring	Mechanism: Spring	Mechanism: Spring
Height: 2"	Height: 2.25"	Height: 1.75"
Value Index: 3	Value Index: 5	Value Index: 5

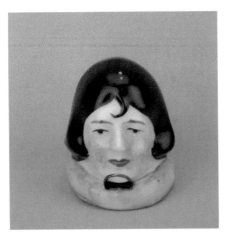

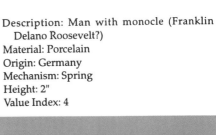

Description: Man with monocle (Franklin
Delano Roosevelt?)
Material: Porcelain
Origin: Germany
Mechanism: Spring
Height: 2"
Value Index: 4

Description: Lady with curl
Material: Porcelain
Origin: Germany
Mechanism: Spring
Height: 1.5"
Value Index: 5

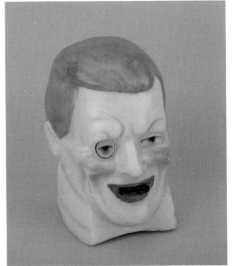

Description: Smiling man (Ronald Coleman?)
Material: Porcelain
Origin: Germany
Mechanism: Spring
Height: 1.75"
Value Index: 3

Description: Scotsman
Material: Porcelain
Origin: Germany
Mechanism: Spring
Height: 2"
Value Index: 5

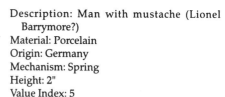

Description: Man with mustache (Lionel
    Barrymore?)
Material: Porcelain
Origin: Germany
Mechanism: Spring
Height: 2"
Value Index: 5

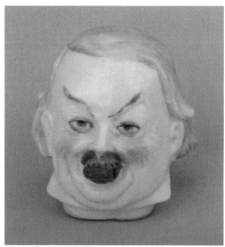

Description: Japanese lady
Material: Plaster of paris
Origin: Unknown
Mechanism: Spring
Height: 2"
Value Index: 5

Description: Aviator
Material: Porcelain
Origin: Germany
Mechanism: Spring
Height: 2"
Value Index: 4

Description: Indian
Material: Porcelain
Origin: Germany
Mechanism: Spring
Height: 2.25"
Value Index: 4

Chapter 3
Animal figures

There are many different animal tape measures, from common cats and dogs to unusual snakes and rats. Birds were favorite subjects of the tapes and over thirty different varieties are pictured. As with the human tape measures, the animals are divided into "Full Figure" and "Heads" for easy reference. "Full Figure" animals are more commonly portrayed than the heads.

Below left
Description: Owl on tape casing
Material: White metal
Origin: Unknown
Mechanism: Spring
Height: 2"
Value Index: 4

Below center
Description: Owl with cigar
Material: Celluloid
Origin: Unknown
Mechanism: Spring
Height: 2.5"
Value Index: 4

Below right
Description: Owl with collapsible winder
Material: White metal
Origin: "London Made Austria"
Mechanism: Wind-up
Height: 1.75"
Value Index: 4

Description: Kangaroo
Material: White metal
Origin: Unknown
Mechanism: Spring
Height: 3.75"
Value Index: 5

Description: Owl on 3-pronged base
Material: Brass, agate
Origin: Unknown
Mechanism: Wind-up
Height: 2.25"
Value Index: 4

Description: Owl
Material: Brass
Origin: Germany
Mechanism: Spring
Height: 2.25"
Value Index: 4

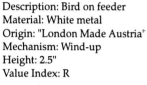

Description: Bird on feeder
Material: White metal
Origin: "London Made Austria"
Mechanism: Wind-up
Height: 2.5"
Value Index: R

Description: Bird in cage
Material: Brass
Origin: Unknown
Mechanism: Wind-up
Height: 2.75"
Value Index: 5

Description: Bird in cage (two color variations)
Material: Brass, celluloid
Origin: Germany
Mechanism: Spring
Height: 1.5"
Value Index: 3

Description: Bird with amethyst
Material: Brass
Origin: Unknown
Mechanism: Wind-up
Height: 1.25"
Value Index: 3

Description: Bird in square cage
Material: Brass
Origin: Germany
Mechanism: Wind-up
Height: 2.5"
Value Index: 3

Description: Chick with worm (two variations)
Material: Brass; brass and celluloid
Origin: Germany
Mechanism: Wind-up
Height: 1.5"
Value Index: 4

Description: Rooster on stump
Material: Metal
Origin: Unknown
Mechanism: Wind-up
Height: 2"
Value Index: 5

Left
Description: Mallard
Material: White metal
Origin: Unknown
Mechanism: Wind-up
Height: 2"
Value Index: 4

Center
Description: Cockatoo
Material: White metal
Origin: "London Made Austria"
Mechanism: Wind-up
Height: 2"
Value Index: 5

Right
Description: Quail on wood base
Material: Metal, wood
Origin: "London Made Austria"
Mechanism: Wind-up
Height: 1.5"
Value Index: 5

Description: Robin
Material: White metal
Origin: "London Made Austria"
Mechanism: Wind-up
Height: 1.5"
Value Index: 5

Description: Chick with four leaf clover
Material: White metal
Origin: "London Made Austria"
Mechanism: Wind-up
Height: 2.5"
Value Index: 5

Description: Rooster on egg
Material: White metal
Origin: Unknown
Mechanism: Wind-up
Height: 2.25"
Value Index: 5

Description: Toucan
Material: White metal
Origin: Germany
Mechanism: Spring
Height: 2.5"
Value Index:4

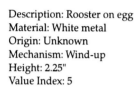

Description: Green woodpecker
Material: Metal
Origin: Germany
Mechanism: Spring
Height: 3"
Value Index: 4

Description: Crows with top
    hats and canes (two color
    variations)
Material: Metal
Origin: Germany
Mechanism: Spring
Height: 5"
Value Index: 4

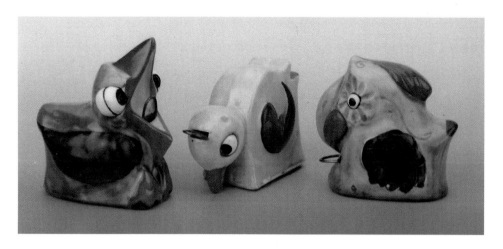

Above left
Description: Bird with open beak
Material: Porcelain
Origin: Germany
Mechanism: Spring
Height: 2.25"
Value Index: 4

Above center
Description: Chick pecking at ground
Material: Porcelain
Origin: Unknown
Mechanism: Spring
Height: 1.5"
Value Index: 3

Above right
Description: Rooster
Material: Porcelain
Origin: Unknown
Mechanism: Spring
Height: 2"
Value Index: 4

Description: Parrot on branch
Material: Stippled celluloid
Origin: Unknown
Mechanism: Spring
Height: 3"
Value Index: 4

Description: Sandpiper (three color variations)
Material: Stippled celluloid
Origin: Unknown
Mechanism: Spring
Height: 2.5"
Value Index: 4

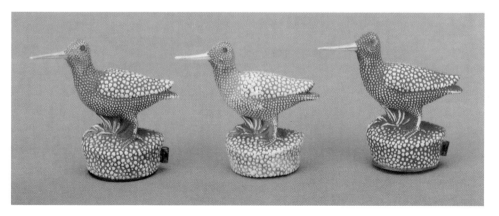

Description: Duck on a tree stump
Material: White metal
Origin: "London Made Austria"
Mechanism: Wind-up
Height: 2"
Value Index: 5

Description: Turkey
Material: Celluloid
Origin: Unknown
Mechanism: Spring
Height: 2.75"
Value Index: 4

Description: Mallard duck
Material: Celluloid
Origin: Unknown
Mechanism: Spring
Height: 1.75"
Value Index: 4

Below left
Description: Cockatoo on base
Material: Celluloid
Origin: Germany
Mechanism: Spring
Height: 2.5"
Value Index: 4

Below right
Description: Cockatoo on ball
Material: Celluloid
Origin: Germany
Mechanism: Spring
Height: 2.25"
Value Index: 4

Description: Mallard on base
Material: Celluloid
Origin: Unknown
Mechanism: Spring
Height: 2.5"
Value Index: 4

Left
Description: Hen with chicks
Material: Celluloid
Origin: Japan
Mechanism: Spring
Height: 1.5"
Value Index: 3

Center
Description: Chick hatching from egg
Material: Celluloid
Origin: Unknown
Mechanism: Spring
Height: 1.5"
Value Index: 4

Right
Description: Two chicks in basket
Material: Celluloid
Origin: Unknown
Mechanism: Spring
Height: 2"
Value Index: 3

Description: Swan on base
Material: Celluloid, bakelite
Origin: Germany
Mechanism: Spring
Height: 2"
Value Index: 3

Left
Description: Flying bird
Material: Celluloid
Origin: Unknown
Mechanism: Spring
Height: 1.5"
Value Index: 3

Center
Description: Parrot on limb
Material: Celluloid
Origin: Unknown
Mechanism: Spring
Height: 1.5"
Value Index: 3

Right
Description: Flying bird
Material: Celluloid
Origin: Unknown
Mechanism: Spring
Height: 1.25"
Value Index: 3

Description: Swan on base
Material: Celluloid
Origin: Japan
Mechanism: Spring
Height: 2"
Value Index: 2

Left
Description: Duckling
Material: Celluloid
Origin: Unknown
Mechanism: Spring
Height: 2.75"
Value Index: 2

Center
Description: Pelican
Material: Plastic
Origin: Japan
Mechanism: Spring
Height: 2.5"
Value Index: 2

Right
Description: Chick with open wings
Material: Celluloid
Origin: Japan
Mechanism: Spring
Height: 2.5"
Value Index: 2

Description: Birds on wall
Material: Celluloid
Origin: Japan
Mechanism: Spring
Height: 2.25"
Value Index: 3

Description: Flamingo
Material: Celluloid
Origin: Japan
Mechanism: Spring
Height: 2.5"
Value Index: 2

Description: Peeping chick
Material: Celluloid
Origin: Occupied Japan
Mechanism: Spring
Height: 2.75"
Value Index: 2

Description: Penguin
Material: Celluloid
Origin: Japan
Mechanism: Spring
Height: 3"
Value Index: 2

Description: 1950s sampler (duck, penguin, rabbit)
Material: Fabric
Origin: Japan
Mechanism: Spring
Height: 1.75"-2.5"
Value Index: 1

Description: Poodle
Material: Brass
Origin: Unknown
Mechanism: Wind-up
Height: 1.75
Value Index: 4

Description: Dachshund on pedestal
Material: White metal
Origin: Unknown
Mechanism: Spring
Height: 1.25"
Value Index: 3

Description: Dog nodder holding drum
Material: Cast iron
Origin: Unknown
Mechanism: Spring
Height: 3"
Value Index: R
Courtesy of Nancy and Benjamin Resnick

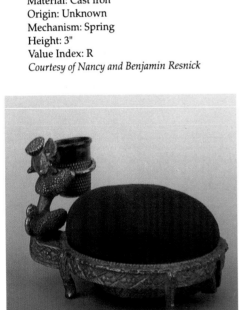

Description: Bulldog begging
Material: Metal
Origin: Unknown
Mechanism: Spring
Height: 2.25
Value Index: 4

Description: Small dog on base
Material: Metal
Origin: Unknown
Mechanism: Spring
Height: 1.75"
Value Index: 3

Description: Poodle with footstool pincushion,
    thimble
Material: Brass
Origin: Unknown
Mechanism: Spring
Height: 2"
Value Index: 2

66

Description: Dog in doghouse (three color variations)
Material: Brass, celluloid
Origin: Germany
Mechanism: Spring
Height: 1.25"
Value Index: 2

Description: Dog in doghouse
Material: Celluloid
Origin: Unknown
Mechanism: Spring
Height: 1.5"
Value Index: 3

Description: Bulldog on stand
Material: Celluloid
Origin: Germany
Mechanism: Spring
Height: 1.75"
Value Index: 3

Description: Dog with shirt, jacket and hat
Material: Celluloid
Origin: Germany
Mechanism: Spring
Height: 2.25"
Value Index: 4

Description: Dog on rock
Material: Celluloid
Origin: Unknown
Mechanism: Spring
Height: 2"
Value Index: 5

67

Left
Description: Puppy
Material: Celluloid
Origin: Germany
Mechanism: Spring
Height: 2.5"
Value Index: 4

Right
Description: Seated bulldog
Material: Celluloid
Origin: Germany
Mechanism: Spring
Height: 2.25"
Value Index: 3

Description: Dagwood's dog Daisy
Material: Celluloid
Origin: Japan
Mechanism: Spring
Height: 2"
Value Index: 3

Description: Shaggy dog on base
Material: Celluloid
Origin: Japan
Mechanism: Spring
Height: 3"
Value Index: 2

Description: Dog on ball (roly-poly)
Material: Celluloid
Origin: Unknown
Mechanism: Spring
Height: 2.5"
Value Index: 3

Left
Description: Dog and puppy on cushion
Material: Celluloid
Origin: Japan
Mechanism: Spring
Height: 2"
Value Index: 2

Left center
Description: Two dogs in basket
Material: Celluloid
Origin: Japan
Mechanism: Spring
Height: 2.5"
Value Index: 2

Right center
Description: Dog on round box
Material: Celluloid
Origin: Japan
Mechanism: Spring
Height: 2.25"
Value Index: 2

Right
Description: Dog on stump
Material: Celluloid
Origin: Unknown
Mechanism: Spring
Height: 2.25"
Value Index: 2

Left
Description: Seated spaniel
Material: Celluloid
Origin: Japan
Mechanism: Spring
Height: 2.5"
Value Index: 2

Center
Description: Seated scotty
Material: Celluloid
Origin: Japan
Mechanism: Spring
Height: 2.25"
Value Index: 2

Right
Description: Seated spaniel
Material: Celluloid
Origin: Japan
Mechanism: Spring
Height: 2.5"
Value Index: 2

Left, Center
Description: Waving dog (two color variations)
Material: Celluloid
Origin: Japan
Mechanism: Spring
Height: 2.75"
Value Index: 2

Right
Description: Sitting dog with collar
Material: Celluloid
Origin: Japan
Mechanism: Spring
Height: 2.75"
Value Index: 2

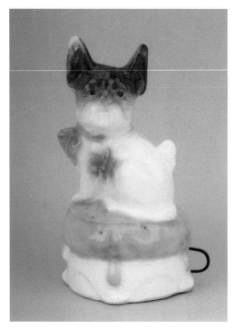

Description: Dog
Material: Porcelain
Origin: Germany
Mechanism: Spring
Height: 2.75"
Value Index: 3

Description: Dog on stuffed stool
Material: Porcelain
Origin: Germany
Mechanism: Spring
Height: 3.25"
Value Index: 4

Above left
Description: Turtle, "Old South Church" scene
Material: Sterling
Origin: Unknown
Mechanism: Spring
Height: 0.5" (2.25" length)
Value Index: 4

Above center
Description: Turtle, nature scene in relief
Material: Metal
Origin: Unknown
Mechanism: Spring
Height: 0.5" (2.5" length)
Value Index: 3

Above right
Description: Turtle, "The New Library of Congress"
Material: Sterling
Origin: Unknown
Mechanism: Spring
Height: 0.5" (2.5" length)
Value Index: 4

Below left
Description: Turtle, "Other Turtles Have Four Feet I Have Seven"
Material: Metal
Origin: Unknown
Mechanism: Spring
Height: 0.5" (2.5" length)
Value Index: 3

Below right:
Description: Turtle, "Pull My Head Not My Leg"
Material: Metal
Origin: Unknown
Mechanism: Spring
Height: 0.5" (2.5" length)
Value Index: 3

Description: Turtle (two color variations)
Material: Celluloid
Origin: Germany
Mechanism: Spring
Height: 0.5" (2.25" length)
Value Index: 3

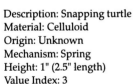

Description: Snapping turtle
Material: Celluloid
Origin: Unknown
Mechanism: Spring
Height: 1" (2.5" length)
Value Index: 3

Description: Turtle (two color variations)
Material: White metal
Origin: Unknown
Mechanism: Wind-up
Height: 1"
Value Index: 3

Description: Turtle with drawn legs (two color variations)
Material: Brass
Origin: Germany
Mechanism: Wind-up
Height: 0.75"
Value Index: 4

Description: Box turtle
Material: Celluloid
Origin: Unknown
Mechanism: Spring
Height: 0.5" (2.75" length)
Value Index: 3

Description: Frog
Material: Celluloid
Origin: Unknown
Mechanism: Spring
Height: 1" (2.5" length)
Value Index: 3

Below left
Description: Frog
Material: Celluloid
Origin: Unknown
Mechanism: Spring
Height: 1.25"
Value Index: 3

Below right
Description: Frog with fly
Material: Celluloid
Origin: Germany
Mechanism: Spring
Height: 1"
Value Index: 3

Description: Frog
Material: Celluloid
Origin: Unknown
Mechanism: Spring
Height: 1" (2.25" length)
Value Index: 3

Description: Alligator
Material: Metal
Origin: Unknown
Mechanism: Spring
Height: 2"
Value Index: 4

Left
Description: Alligator with open jaws
Material: White metal
Origin: Unknown
Mechanism: Spring
Height: 2.75"
Value Index: 4

Right
Description: Frog
Material: White metal
Origin: Unknown
Mechanism: Spring
Height: 2.25"
Value Index: 3

Description: Alligator with jaw pull
Material: Celluloid
Origin: Japan
Mechanism: Spring
Height: 1" (7.5" length)
Value Index: 3

Description: Alligator with black head in mouth
Material: Celluloid
Origin: Japan
Mechanism: Spring
Height: 1.75" (6" length)
Value Index: 4

Description: Flounder
Material: Metal
Origin: Unknown
Mechanism: Spring
Height: 1.5"
Value Index: 2

Description: Alligator with fish in mouth
Material: Celluloid
Origin: Germany
Mechanism: Spring
Height: 0.75" (6" length)
Value Index: 5

Description: Flounder
Material: Celluloid
Origin: Germany
Mechanism: Spring
Height: 2"
Value Index: 4

Description: Angel fish
Material: Celluloid
Origin: Unknown
Mechanism: Spring
Height: 2.5"
Value Index: 3

Left
Description: Goldfish
Material: Celluloid
Origin: Japan
Mechanism: Spring
Height: 1" (3" length)
Value Index: 1

Right
Description: Red fish
Material: Celluloid
Origin: Unknown
Mechanism: Spring
Height: 1.25" (4" length)
Value Index: 2

Left front
Description: Wide-mouth bass
Material: Celluloid
Origin: Japan
Mechanism: Spring
Height: 4" (length)
Value Index: 2

Right front
Description: Bass fish
Material: Plastic
Origin: Japan
Mechanism: Spring
Height: 1.75"
Value Index: 1

Left back
Description: Swordfish
Material: Plastic
Origin: Japan
Mechanism: Spring
Height: 1"
Value Index: 1

Right back
Description: Speckled bass
Material: Celluloid
Origin: Japan
Mechanism: Spring
Height: 1" (4" length)
Value Index: 1

Description: Pig on dice
Material: White metal, brass
Origin: Unknown
Mechanism: Wind-up
Height: 1.5"
Value Index: 3

Description: Black pig
Material: Metal
Origin: Unknown
Mechanism: Wind-up
Height: 1.5"
Value Index: 3

Left
Description: Pig
Material: Brass
Origin: Germany
Mechanism: Wind-up
Height: 1"
Value Index: 3

Right
Description: Pig
Material: White metal
Origin: Unknown
Mechanism: Wind-up
Height: 1"
Value Index: 3

Description: Boar
Material: White metal
Origin: Unknown
Mechanism: Spring
Height: 1.25"
Value Index: 3

Description: Pig in shoe (two color variations)
Material: Celluloid
Origin: Japan
Mechanism: Spring
Height: 2"
Value Index: 1

Description: Pig with hat (three color variations)
Material: Celluloid
Origin: Japan
Mechanism: Spring
Height: 1.5"
Value Index: 1

Description: Flat pig
Material: Celluloid
Origin: Unknown
Mechanism: Spring
Height: 1.25"
Value Index: 1

Left
Description: Pig
Material: Celluloid
Origin: Japan
Mechanism: Spring
Height: 1.5"
Value Index: 1

Right
Description: Pig with piglet
Material: Celluloid
Origin: Japan
Mechanism: Spring
Height: 1.5"
Value Index: 1

Description: Winking pig
Material: Celluloid
Origin: Japan
Mechanism: Spring
Height: 1.5"
Value Index: 1

Description: Elephant on stand
Material: Celluloid
Origin: Unknown
Mechanism: Spring
Height: 1.75"
Value Index: 3

Description: Pig with closed eyes
Material: Celluloid
Origin: Japan
Mechanism: Spring
Height: 1.5"
Value Index: 1

Description: Elephant with ivory tusks
Material: Celluloid, ivory
Origin: Unknown
Mechanism: Spring
Height: 2.5"
Value Index: 4

Left
Description: Elephant on platform
Material: Celluloid
Origin: Germany
Mechanism: Spring
Height: 1.25"
Value Index: 3

Center
Description: Elephant on round striped stand
Material: Celluloid
Origin: Unknown
Mechanism: Spring
Height: 1.25"
Value Index: 3

Right
Description: Elephant on base
Material: Celluloid
Origin: Unknown
Mechanism: Spring
Height: 1.5"
Value Index: 3

Description: Elephant with ivory tusks
Material: Brass
Origin: Unknown
Mechanism: Wind-up
Height: 1.5"
Value Index: 5

Left
Description: Elephant
Material: Celluloid
Origin: Japan
Mechanism: Spring
Height: 3"
Value Index: 2

Right
Description: Elephant
Material: Celluloid
Origin: Japan
Mechanism: Spring
Height: 2.25"
Value Index: 2

Left
Description: Elephant with rhinestones
Material: Celluloid
Origin: Japan
Mechanism: Spring
Height: 2"
Value Index: 1

Right
Description: Elephant with beads
Material: Celluloid
Origin: Japan
Mechanism: Spring
Height: 2"
Value Index: 1

Description: Elephant with chair and rider
Material: Celluloid
Origin: Unknown
Mechanism: Spring
Height: 2"
Value Index: 3

Description: Elephant on black base
Material: Celluloid
Origin: Unknown
Mechanism: Spring
Height: 1.5"
Value Index: 2

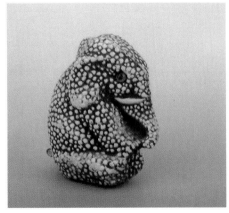

Description: Sitting elephant
Material: Stippled celluloid
Origin: Germany
Mechanism: Spring
Height: 2"
Value Index: 4

Description: Elephant in relief
Material: Celluloid
Origin: Unknown
Mechanism: Spring
Height: 1.75"
Value Index: 2

Description: Sitting rabbit and basket (also pin-
   cushion)
Material: Metal
Origin: Unknown
Mechanism: Spring
Height: 1.5"
Value Index: 4

Description: Rabbit
Material: Brass/celluloid
Origin: Germany
Mechanism: Wind-up
Height: 2"
Value Index: 3

Description: Sitting rabbit
Material: Metal
Origin: Unknown
Mechanism: Wind-up
Height: 2"
Value Index: 5

Description: Easter bunny on basket
Material: White metal
Origin: Unknown
Mechanism: Wind-up
Height: 2.5"
Value Index: 4

Left
Description: Rabbit with large egg
Material: Celluloid
Origin: Germany
Mechanism: Spring
Height: 2.5"
Value Index: 4

Center
Description: Rabbit with two baskets of colored
    eggs
Material: Celluloid
Origin: Germany
Mechanism: Spring
Height: 2.25"
Value Index: 4

Right
Description: Rabbit with carrot
Material: Celluloid
Origin: Germany
Mechanism: Spring
Height: 2"
Value Index: 4

Description: Rabbit
Material: Stippled celluloid
Origin: Unknown
Mechanism: Spring
Height: 1.25"
Value Index: 4

Description: Cat on base (holds thimble and
    needles)
Material: Bakelite
Origin: Unknown
Mechanism: Spring
Height: 3.75"
Value Index: 1

Description: Black cat
Material: Celluloid
Origin: Germany
Mechanism: Spring
Height: 1.5"
Value Index: 4

Left
Description: Standing rabbit
Material: Celluloid
Origin: Occupied Japan
Mechanism: Spring
Height: 2.5"
Value Index: 2

Right
Description: Rabbit on haunches
Material: Celluloid
Origin: Japan
Mechanism: Spring
Height: 3.25"
Value Index: 2

Description: Cat
Material: Brass
Origin: Unknown
Mechanism: Wind-up
Height: 1.75"
Value Index: 4

Description: Cat holding thimble in ring
Material: White metal
Origin: France
Mechanism: Wind-up
Height: 2.5"
Value Index: 5

Description: Cat on roller skates
Material: Celluloid
Origin: France
Mechanism: Wind-up
Height: 4.75"
Value Index: R

83

Description: Cat with ball
Material: Vienna bronze/brass
Origin: Unknown
Mechanism: Wind-up
Height: 1.5"
Value Index: 5

Description: Cat
Material: Metal
Origin: Unknown
Mechanism: Wind-up
Height: 3"
Value Index: R

Description: Cat with collapsible winder
Material: White metal
Origin: "London Made Austria"
Mechanism: Wind-up
Height: 2"
Value Index: 4

Description: Waving cat
Material: Celluloid
Origin: Japan, Occupied Japan
Mechanism: Spring
Height: 2.5"
Value Index: 1

Description: Bear with barrel (thimble holder)
Material: Celluloid
Origin: Germany
Mechanism: Spring
Height: 2"
Value Index: 4

Description: Bear with muzzle, pole, and nose ring
Material: Celluloid
Origin: Unknown
Mechanism: Spring
Height: 4"
Value Index: 5

Description: Bear on all fours (two color variations)
Material: Celluloid
Origin: Japan
Mechanism: Spring
Height: 1.25"
Value Index: 2

Description: Teddy bear
Material: Celluloid
Origin: Occupied Japan
Mechanism: Spring
Height: 3"
Value Index: 1

Description: Cow on base
Material: Plastic
Origin: Japan
Mechanism: Spring
Height: 1.75"
Value Index: 2

Description: Bull
Material: Celluloid
Origin: Unknown
Mechanism: Spring
Height: 2.75"
Value Index: 5

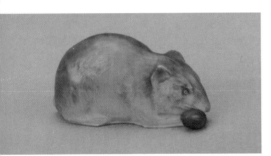

Description: Mouse with nut
Material: Celluloid
Origin: Unknown
Mechanism: Spring
Height: 1.25"
Value Index: 4

Description: Cow with fly
Material: Celluloid
Origin: Germany
Mechanism: Spring
Height: 1.75"
Value Index: 5

Description: Mouse
Material: Metal
Origin: Unknown
Mechanism: Wind-up
Height: 1"
Value Index: 5

Description: Rats on boot
Material: Celluloid
Origin: Unknown
Mechanism: Spring
Height: 1.75"
Value Index: 4

Description: Rat with carrot
Material: Celluloid
Origin: Unknown
Mechanism: Spring
Height: 1"
Value Index: 4

Description: Ladybug
Material: Celluloid
Origin: Unknown
Mechanism: Spring
Height: 0.75" (2" length)
Value Index: 3

Description: Beetle
Material: Celluloid
Origin: Unknown
Mechanism: Spring
Height: 3"
Value Index: 5

Left
Description: Butterfly on base (red)
Material: Celluloid
Origin: Unknown
Mechanism: Spring
Height: 1.75" x 1.50" (width x length)
Value Index: 4

Description: Fly on egg
Material: Celluloid
Origin: Unknown
Mechanism: Japan
Height: 0.75" (1.5" length)
Value Index: 2

Right
Description: Butterfly on base (cream)
Material: Celluloid
Origin: Unknown
Mechanism: Spring
Height: 2.5" (wingspan)
Value Index: 3

Left
Description: Squirrel with acorn at stomach
Material: Celluloid
Origin: Japan
Mechanism: Spring
Height: 2.5"
Value Index: 2

Right
Description: Squirrel with acorn at mouth
Material: Celluloid
Origin: Japan
Mechanism: Spring
Height: 2"
Value Index: 2

Description: Beehive
Material: Brass
Origin: Unknown
Mechanism: Wind-up
Height: 2.25"
Value Index: 5

Description: Squirrel with nut (replaced nut)
Material: Brass
Origin: Unknown
Mechanism: Wind-up
Height: 2.75"
Value Index: 5

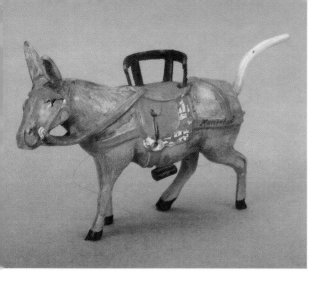

Description: Burro with saddle
Material: Celluloid
Origin: Germany
Mechanism: Wind-up
Height: 2.5"
Value Index: 5

Description: Calf on rock
Material: Celluloid
Origin: Unknown
Mechanism: Spring
Height: 2.25"
Value Index: 5

Description:
Sheep on rock
Material: Cellu-
loid
Origin: Unknown
Mechanism:
Spring
Height: 2.25"
Value Index: 4

Description: Ram on rock
Material: Celluloid
Origin: Unknown
Mechanism: Spring
Height: 2.5"
Value Index: 4

Description: Donkey
Material: Metal
Origin: Unknown
Mechanism: Wind-up
Height: 3"
Value Index: R

Description: Donkey
Material: Brass
Origin: Germany
Mechanism: Wind-up
Height: 2.25"
Value Index: 3

Description: Monkey
Material: Brass
Origin: Unknown
Mechanism: Wind-up
Height: 2.25"
Value Index: 4

Description: Sitting donkey
Material: Celluloid
Origin: Unknown
Mechanism: Spring
Height: 2.75"
Value Index: 5

Description: Donkey on cushion
Material: Celluloid
Origin: Japan
Mechanism: Spring
Height: 2.25"
Value Index: 3

Description: Monkey on a tree stump
Material: White metal
Origin: "London Made Austria"
Mechanism: Wind-up
Height: 1.5"
Value Index: 5

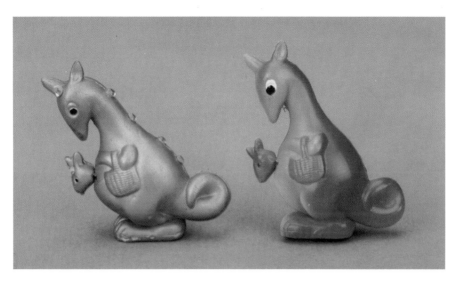

Description: Kangaroo with joey (two color
    variations)
Material: Celluloid
Origin: Japan
Mechanism: Spring
Height: 2.75"
Value Index: 1

Left
Description: Snail
Material: Celluloid
Origin: Japan
Mechanism: Spring
Height: 1.5"
Value Index: 3

Right
Description: Fawn
Material: Plastic
Origin: Japan
Mechanism: Spring
Height: 2"
Value Index: 1

Description: Snail
Material: Celluloid
Origin: Germany
Mechanism: Spring
Height: 1.25"
Value Index: 4

Description: Rattlesnake
Material: Celluloid
Origin: Unknown
Mechanism: Spring
Height: 1" (3.25" length)
Value Index: 4

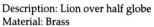

Description: Lion over half globe
Material: Brass
Origin: Unknown
Mechanism: Wind-up
Height: 2"
Value Index: 4

Description: Giraffe
Material: Celluloid (resin?)
Origin: Unknown
Mechanism: Spring
Height: 5.5"
Value Index: 5

Description: German Shepherd
Material: Celluloid
Origin: Unknown
Mechanism: Spring
Height: 1.75"
Value Index: 4

Description: Dog with pilot hat and goggles
Material: White metal
Origin: Unknown
Mechanism: Spring
Height: 2.25"
Value Index: 5

Description: Terrier
Material: Celluloid
Origin: Germany
Mechanism: Spring
Height: 1.5"
Value Index: 4

Description: Bonzo (original tongue missing)
Material: Celluloid
Origin: Unknown
Mechanism: Spring
Height: 1.5"
Value Index: 4

Description: Bulldog with fly
Material: Porcelain
Origin: Unknown
Mechanism: Spring
Height: 1.75"
Value Index: 4

Description: Bulldog
Material: Celluloid
Origin: Germany
Mechanism: Spring
Height: 1.5"
Value Index: 4

Left
Description: Bulldog
Material: Celluloid
Origin: Japan
Mechanism: Spring
Height: 1.5"
Value Index: 4

Right
Description: Bulldog (tan)
Material: Celluloid
Origin: Japan
Mechanism: Spring
Height: 1.5"
Value Index: 4

Description: Bulldog with hat
Material: Celluloid
Origin: Germany
Mechanism: Spring
Height: 2"
Value Index: 4

Left
Description: Hound with collar
Material: Celluloid
Origin: Unknown
Mechanism: Spring
Height: 1.25"
Value Index: 3

Right
Description: Hound with glass eyes
Material: Celluloid
Origin: Unknown
Mechanism: Spring
Height: 1.25"
Value Index: 3

Description: Wolf
Material: Celluloid
Origin: Unknown
Mechanism: Spring
Height: 1.5"
Value Index: 3

Description: Duck holding fly in beak
Material: Celluloid
Origin: Unknown
Mechanism: Spring
Height: 1.75"
Value Index: 4

Description: Rooster
Material: Celluloid
Origin: Unknown
Mechanism: Spring
Height: 2.25"
Value Index: 5

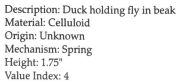

Left
Description: Cockatoo
Material: Celluloid
Origin: Unknown
Mechanism: Spring
Height: 1.5"
Value Index: 4

Right
Description: Parrot
Material: Celluloid
Origin: Germany
Mechanism: Spring
Height: 1.25"
Value Index: 4

Description: Owl with glass eyes
Material: Celluloid
Origin: Unknown
Mechanism: Spring
Height: 1.5"
Value Index: 4

Description: Owl
Material: Porcelain
Origin: Germany
Mechanism: Spring
Height: 1.25"
Value Index: 5

Description: Monkey
Material: Celluloid
Origin: Unknown
Mechanism: Spring
Height: 1.5"
Value Index: 3

Description: Owl
Material: Metal
Origin: "London Made In Austria"
Mechanism: Wind-up
Height: 1.25"
Value Index: 5

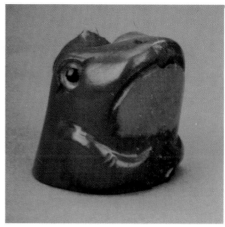

Description: Frog (also pincushion)
Material: Wood
Origin: Unknown
Mechanism: Spring
Height: 2.25"
Value Index: 1

Description: Monkey with fez
Material: Plastic
Origin: Japan
Mechanism: Spring
Height: 2"
Value Index: 2

Description: Porky Pig
Material: Plastic
Origin: Japan
Mechanism: Spring
Height: 1.75"
Value Index: 1

Description: Relief of cat
Material: Celluloid
Origin: Germany
Mechanism: Spring
Height: 1.25"
Value Index: 3

Description: Ram
Material: Celluloid
Origin: Unknown
Mechanism: Spring
Height: 3"
Value Index: 5

Description: Cat
Material: Porcelain
Origin: Germany
Mechanism: Spring
Height: 2"
Value Index: 4

Description: Relief of elephant
Material: Celluloid
Origin: Germany
Mechanism: Spring
Height: 1.25"
Value Index: 3

Top right
Description: Relief of owl with glass eyes
Material: Brass
Origin: Germany
Mechanism: Spring with button
Height: 1.25"
Value Index: 1

Center right
Description: Relief of Irish setter
Material: Brass
Origin: Germany
Mechanism: Spring
Height: 1.25"
Value Index: 2

Bottom
Description: Relief of horse
Material: Brass, glass eyes
Origin: Germany
Mechanism: Spring
Height: 1.25"
Value Index: 2

Center left
Description: Relief of bulldog
Material: Brass, glass eyes
Origin: Germany
Mechanism: Spring
Height: 1.25"
Value Index: 2

Top left
Description: Relief of cat
Material: Brass, glass eyes
Origin: Germany
Mechanism: Spring
Height: 1.25"
Value Index: 2

Chapter 5
Fruits, vegetables, and flowers

The fruit and flower tape measures are most commonly portrayed in baskets or bunches. Individual fruits, flowers, and vegetables, however, are also seen, often with a fly or ladybug as the end of the tape. As with other categories, the tape measures in this group were made in all materials, but the majority were celluloid.

Description: Bunch of daisies
Material: Celluloid
Origin: Germany
Mechanism: Spring
Height: 2.25"
Value Index: 3

Description: Flowers in basket
Material: Celluloid, fabric
Origin: Unknown
Mechanism: Spring
Height: 3.5"
Value Index: 4

Left
Description: Lilies of the valley
Material: Celluloid
Origin: Unknown
Mechanism: Spring
Height: 2"
Value Index: 3

Center
Description: Pink dogwood
Material: Celluloid
Origin: Unknown
Mechanism: Spring
Height: 2"
Value Index: 2

Right
Description: Thistles
Material: Celluloid
Origin: Unknown
Mechanism: Spring
Height: 2"
Value Index: 3

Left
Description: Tulip
Material: Celluloid
Origin: Germany
Mechanism: Spring
Height: 2"
Value Index: 2

Center
Description: Two bluebells
Material: Celluloid
Origin: Unknown
Mechanism: Spring
Height: 2"
Value Index: 2

Right
Description: Red tulip
Material: Celluloid
Origin: Germany
Mechanism: Spring
Height: 1.5"
Value Index: 2

Left	*Center*	*Right*
Description: Sunflower	Description: Pansy, low vase	Description: Dogwood with bud
Material: Celluloid	Material: Celluloid	Material: Celluloid
Origin: Unknown	Origin: Germany	Origin: Unknown
Mechanism: Spring	Mechanism: Spring	Mechanism: Spring
Height: 1.75"	Height: 2"	Height: 2.25"
Value Index: 2	Value Index: 2	Value Index: 3

Left	*Center*	*Right*
Description: Red rose with bud	Description: Primrose	Description: Currents
Material: Celluloid	Material: Celluloid	Material: Celluloid
Origin: Unknown	Origin: Unknown	Origin: Unknown
Mechanism: Spring	Mechanism: Spring	Mechanism: Spring
Height: 2"	Height: 1.5"	Height: 2"
Value Index: 3	Value Index: 3	Value Index: 3

Description: Three pansies on base (two color
   variations)
Material: Celluloid
Origin: Germany
Mechanism: Spring
Height:1.75"
Value Index: 2

Left
Description: Flaring flower basket
Material: Celluloid
Origin: Germany
Mechanism: Spring
Height: 1.5"
Value Index: 2

Right
Description: Flaring fruit basket
Material: Celluloid
Origin: Germany
Mechanism: Spring
Height: 1.5"
Value Index: 2

Left
Description: Fruit basket with low handle
Material: Celluloid
Origin: Japan
Mechanism: Spring
Height: 1.75"
Value Index: 2

Center
Description: Flower basket with high handle
Material: Celluloid
Origin: Japan
Mechanism: Spring
Height: 2"
Value Index: 2

Right
Description: Fruit basket with high handle
Material: Celluloid
Origin: Japan
Mechanism: Spring
Height: 2"
Value Index: 2

Description: Mixed flowers in pot with two
   handles
Material: Celluloid
Origin: Japan
Mechanism: Spring
Height: 1.5"
Value Index: 2

Description: Flower basket with partly opened
   lid
Material: Celluloid
Origin: Japan
Mechanism: Spring
Height: 1.5"
Value Index: 2

Left
Description: Oval flower basket with overhang-
   ing blossoms
Material: Celluloid
Origin: Unknown
Mechanism: Spring
Height: 1.75"
Value Index: 2

Right
Description: Oval flower basket
Material: Celluloid
Origin: Unknown
Mechanism: Spring
Height: 1.5"
Value Index: 2

Description: Flowers in
   deep vase with deco-
   ration (two color
   variations)
Material: Celluloid
Origin: Unknown
Mechanism: Spring
Height: 1.5"
Value Index: 2

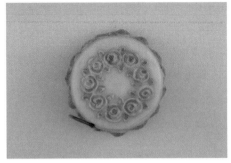

Description: Flower basket (also pincushion)
Material: Celluloid
Origin: Unknown
Mechanism: Spring
Height: 1.5"
Value Index: 2

Description: Reliefs of roses (cake top?)
Material: Celluloid
Origin: Unknown
Mechanism: Spring
Height: 0.75"
Value Index: 2

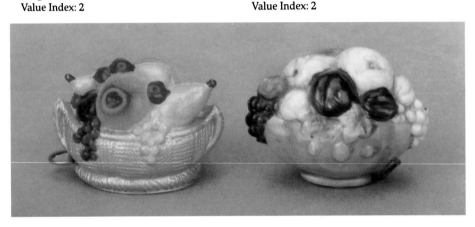

Left
Description: Fruit in oval basket
Material: Celluloid
Origin: Japan
Mechanism: Spring
Height: 1.25"
Value Index: 2

Right
Description: Fruit in deep basket
Material: Celluloid
Origin: Japan
Mechanism: Spring
Height: 1.5"
Value Index: 2

Description: Fruit bowl with pedestal
Material: Celluloid
Origin: Germany
Mechanism: Spring
Height: 1.5"
Value Index: 3

Left
Description: Woven round fruit basket
Material: Celluloid
Origin: Germany
Mechanism: Spring
Height: 1.25"
Value Index: 2

Right
Description: Woven round fruit basket
Material: Celluloid
Origin: Japan
Mechanism: Spring
Height: 1.25"
Value Index: 2

Description: Apple ("You Are The Apple of My
Eye" on tape)
Material: Metal
Origin: Japan
Mechanism: Spring
Height: 2"
Value Index: 1

Left
Description: Plum with fly
Material: Celluloid
Origin: Germany
Mechanism: Spring
Height: 2"
Value Index: 3

Right
Description: Apple with fly
Material: Celluloid
Origin: Germany
Mechanism: Spring
Height: 1.75"
Value Index: 3

Description: Apple (tape missing)
Material: Celluloid
Origin: Unknown
Mechanism: Spring
Height: 1"
Value Index: 2

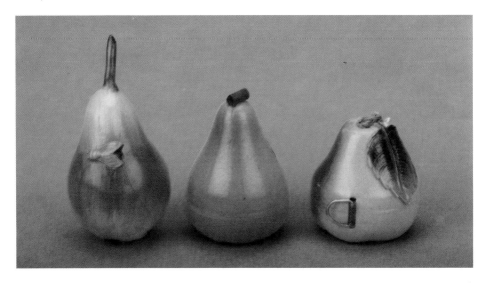

Left
Description: Pear with fly
Material: Celluloid
Origin: Germany
Mechanism: Spring
Height: 2.5"
Value Index: 3

Center
Description: Pear
Material: Celluloid
Origin: Unknown
Mechanism: Spring
Height: 1.75"
Value Index: 1

Right
Description: Pear
Material: Celluloid
Origin: Unknown
Mechanism: Spring
Height: 1.5"
Value Index: 3

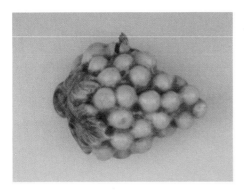

Description: Grapes with ladybug
Material: Celluloid
Origin: Unknown
Mechanism: Spring
Height: 2"
Value Index: 3

Description: Melon
Material: Celluloid
Origin: Unknown
Mechanism: Spring
Height: 1.25"
Value Index: 2

Description: Tomato
Material: Composition
Origin: Japan
Mechanism: Spring
Height: 1.5"
Value Index: 2

106

Left, Right
Description: Strawberry (two color variations)
Material: Celluloid
Origin: Unknown
Mechanism: Spring
Height: 1.75"
Value Index: 3

Center
Description: Lemon
Material: Celluloid
Origin: Unknown
Mechanism: Spring
Height: 2"
Value Index: 2

Description: Opening chestnut
Material: Celluloid
Origin: Unknown
Mechanism: Spring
Height: 1.5"
Value Index: 3

Description: Lemon
Material: Composition
Origin: Japan
Mechanism: Spring
Height: 1.5"
Value Index: 2

Description: Turnip
Material: Celluloid
Origin: Unknown
Mechanism: Spring
Height: 2.5"
Value Index: 3

Left
Description: Cauliflower
Material: Celluloid
Origin: Germany
Mechanism: Spring
Height: 1.75"
Value Index: 3

Right
Description: Melon
Material: Celluloid
Origin: Germany
Mechanism: Spring
Height: 1.5"
Value Index: 3

Left
Description: Walnut
Material: Celluloid
Origin: Germany
Mechanism: Spring
Height: 1.5"
Value Index: 2

Center
Description: Hazelnuts
Material: Celluloid
Origin: Unknown
Mechanism: Spring
Height: 2"
Value Index: 3

Right
Description: Walnut
Material: Celluloid
Origin: Unknown
Mechanism: Spring
Height: 2"
Value Index: 2

Description: Acorn
Material: Horn/ivory
Origin: Unknown
Mechanism: Wind-up
Height: 1.5"
Value Index: 4

Description: Cactus
Material: Celluloid
Origin: Unknown
Mechanism: Spring
Height: 2.5"
Value Index: 3

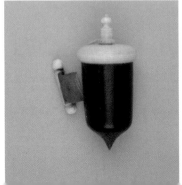

Left
Description: Spiky tree in planter
Material: Brass, metal
Origin: Unknown
Mechanism: Wind-up
Height: 2.75"
Value Index: 5

Description: Thistle (also pincushion)
Material: Brass
Origin: Unknown
Mechanism: Wind-up
Height: 2"
Value Index: 4

Center
Description: Tree with berries in planter
Material: Brass, metal
Origin: Unknown
Mechanism: Wind-up
Height: 2.5"
Value Index: 4
Courtesy of Lucid Antiques, Lucille Malitz

Right
Description: Berry tree in planter
Material: Brass, metal
Origin: Unknown
Mechanism: Wind-up
Height: 2.75"
Value Index: 4

Description: Acorn
Material: Vegetable ivory
Origin: Unknown
Mechanism: Wind-up
Height: 2"
Value Index: 2

109

Chapter 6
Transportation

Cars and boats are the most common subjects for transportation. Also portrayed, however, are less common modes such as dirigibles, hot air balloons, and bicycles. The value index numbers for this category reveal the high collectibility of this subgroup.

Description: Zeppelin
Material: Metal
Origin: Unknown
Mechanism: Wind-up
Height: 1" (3" length)
Value Index: R

Description: Battleship
Material: Celluloid
Origin: Germany
Mechanism: Spring
Height: 1.75" (3" length)
Value Index: 4

Description: Gondola (two color variations)
Material: Celluloid
Origin: Germany
Mechanism: Spring
Height: 1.5" (2.75" length)
Value Index: 3

Left
Description: Ship, crosses on small top flags
Material: Celluloid
Origin: Japan
Mechanism: Spring
Height: 2.25"
Value Index: 2

Center
Description: Ship, marked "DEPOSE" on casing
Material: Celluloid
Origin: Japan
Mechanism: Spring
Height: 2.25"
Value Index: 2

Right
Description: Ship, crosses on large sails
Material: Celluloid
Origin: Japan
Mechanism: Spring
Height: 2.25"
Value Index: 2

Description: Sailboat
Material: Celluloid
Origin: Japan
Mechanism: Spring
Height: 2"
Value Index: 3

Description: Ship on base
Material: Porcelain
Origin: Germany
Mechanism: Spring
Height: 4"
Value Index: 4

111

Description: Three-masted ship (one flag missing)
Material: Metal
Origin: Germany
Mechanism: Spring
Height: 2"
Value Index: 3

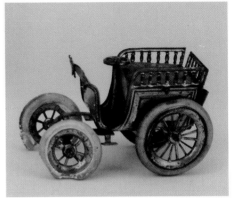

Description: Car
Material: Brass, rubber wheels
Origin: Unknown
Mechanism: Wind-up
Height: 1.5"
Value Index: 5

Description: Car
Material: Brass
Origin: Unknown
Mechanism: Wind-up
Height: 1.5"
Value Index: 4

Description: Coronation coach
Material: Brass, celluloid windows
Origin: Unknown
Mechanism: Wind-up
Height: 1.75"
Value Index: 5

Description: Tin Lizzies (three color variations)
Material: Metal, celluloid windows
Origin: Germany
Mechanism: Spring
Height: 1.25"
Value Index: 3

Description: Conestoga wagon
Material: Celluloid
Origin: Japan
Mechanism: Spring
Height: 1.5"
Value Index: 2

Description: Bathhouse with figure
Material: Brass
Origin: Unknown
Mechanism: Wind-up
Height: 2.5"
Value Index: 5

Description: Bicycle
Material: Metal, ivory
Origin: Unknown
Mechanism: Wind-up
Height: 1.75"
Value Index: 5

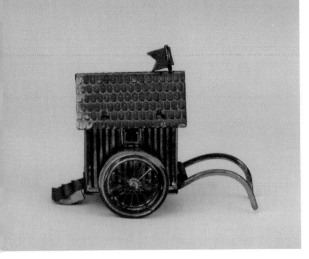

Description: Bathhouse (rickshaw)
Material: Brass
Origin: Unknown
Mechanism: Wind-up
Height: 2.25"
Value Index: 5

Description: Balloon
Material: Brass, celluloid
Origin: Unknown
Mechanism: Wind-up
Height: 2.5"
Value Index: R

Description: Sled with elf
Material: Brass, celluloid
Origin: Unknown
Mechanism: Wind-up
Height: 1.25"
Value Index: 4

Chapter 7
Buildings

There are several famous buildings portrayed in tape measures. St. Peter's Cathedral of London and the Capitol building in Washington D.C. are examples. More usual, however, are the myriad of unidentifiable structures. In this category appear clay tape measures. Clay is a casing material which seems unique to the buildings. Charles Dickens's "The Old Curiosity Shop" is the only easily identifiable clay building.

Left
Description: Cottage with water wheel
Material: Clay
Origin: Unknown
Mechanism: Spring
Height: 2"
Value Index: 4

Center
Description: House with steep roof
Material: Clay
Origin: Unknown
Mechanism: Spring
Height: 2"
Value Index: 4

Right
Description: House with side turret
Material: Clay
Origin: Unknown
Mechanism: Spring
Height: 1.75"
Value Index: 4

Description: Rabbit hutch
Material: Clay
Origin: Unknown
Mechanism: Spring
Height: 1.25"
Value Index: 4

Above left
Description: House with peaked roof
Material: Clay
Origin: Germany
Mechanism: Spring
Height: 2"
Value Index: 4

Above center
Description: House with clock tower
Material: Clay
Origin: Germany
Mechanism: Spring
Height: 2.5"
Value Index: 4

Above right
Description: Squarish house
Material: Clay
Origin: Germany
Mechanism: Spring
Height: 2"
Value Index: 4

Below left
Description: Red-shingled house
Material: Clay
Origin: Germany
Mechanism: Spring
Height: 1.5"
Value Index: 3

Below center
Description: Yellow-roofed house with chimney
Material: Clay
Origin: Germany
Mechanism: Spring
Height: 1.75"
Value Index: 4

Below right
Description: House with two chimneys
Material: Clay
Origin: Unknown
Mechanism: Spring
Height: 1.5"
Value Index: 4

Description: House with trellis (three color variations)
Material: Celluloid
Origin: Unknown
Mechanism: Spring
Height: 1.5"
Value Index: 3

Description: Red-roofed chalet
Material: Celluloid
Origin: Unknown
Mechanism: Spring
Height: 1.5"
Value Index: 2

Description: European-styled house
Material: Celluloid
Origin: Unknown
Mechanism: Spring
Height: 1.5"
Value Index: 3

Description: Swiss chalet
Material: Celluloid
Origin: Unknown
Mechanism: Spring
Height: 1.5"
Value Index: 3

Left
Description: Long house with two roofs
Material: Clay
Origin: Unknown
Mechanism: Spring
Height: 2"
Value Index: 4

Right
Description: The Old Curiosity Shop
Material: Clay
Origin: Unknown
Mechanism: Spring
Height: 1.75"
Value Index: 4

Description: Cottage orné
Material: Wood (Tunbridge ware)
Origin: Unknown
Mechanism: Wind-up
Height: 1"
Value Index: 4

Description: German church
Material: Brass
Origin: Unknown
Mechanism: Wind-up
Height: 3.5"
Value Index: R

Left
Description: St. Paul's Cathedral, London
Material: Celluloid
Origin:Unknown
Mechanism: Spring
Height: 2"
Value Index: 4

Right
Description: Capitol building with dome
Material: Celluloid
Origin: Unknown
Mechanism: Spring
Height: 2.25"
Value Index: 4

Description: Eiffel tower
Material: Metal
Origin: Unknown
Mechanism: Wind-up
Height: 3"
Value Index: 4

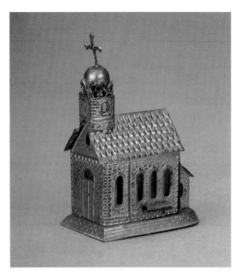

Description: Church with tall steeple
Material: Brass, celluloid
Origin: Unknown
Mechanism: Spring
Height: 3.25"
Value Index: 5

Description: Windmill
Material: Copper
Origin: Unknown
Mechanism: Wind-up
Height: 2.25"
Value Index: 3

Description: Windmill
Material: White metal
Origin: Unknown
Mechanism: Wind-up
Height: 2.75"
Value Index: 5

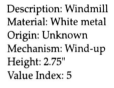

Description: Windmill (two color variations)
Material: Celluloid
Origin: Germany
Mechanism: Spring
Height: 2.5"
Value Index: 3

Description: Windmill (with sewing kit)
Material: Celluloid
Origin: Unknown
Mechanism: Spring
Height: 2.5"
Value Index: 2

Description: Water mill
Material: Brass
Origin: Unknown
Mechanism: Wind-up
Height: 1.5"
Value Index: 4

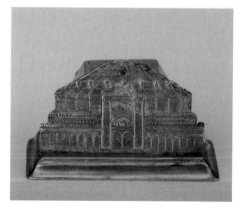

Description: House
Material: Brass
Origin: Unknown
Mechanism: Wind-up
Height: 1.5"
Value Index: 4

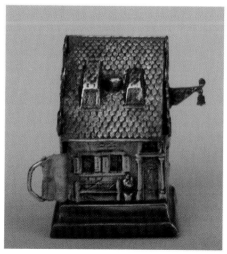

Description: German inn
Material: Brass
Origin: Unknown
Mechanism: Wind-up
Height: 1.75"
Value Index: 4

Description: Capitol Building
Material: Celluloid
Origin: Japan
Mechanism: Spring
Height: 1.75"
Value Index: 3

Description: Lighthouse
Material: Brass
Origin: Unknown
Mechanism: Wind-up
Height: 3"
Value Index: 5

Description: Pyramid with sphinx head
Material: Celluloid
Origin: Unknown
Mechanism: Spring
Height: 1.5"
Value Index: 4

Description: Castle, pincushion in base, marked
    in nails
Material: Rosewood
Origin: Unknown
Mechanism: Wind-up
Height: 2.5"
Value Index: R

Chapter 8
Bells and musical instruments

Types of bells in tape measures vary in style from dinner bells to church bells. Several representations of the Liberty Bell are illustrated. String instruments are well represented with lutes and cellos. The drums are, at times, decorated front and back with hunting or nature scenes. Some tape measures in the shape of music boxes even emit sounds when the tape is wound.

Description: Liberty bell
Material: Celluloid
Origin: Unknown
Mechanism: Spring
Height: 2"
Value Index: 3

Description: Liberty bell
Material: White metal
Origin: Unknown
Mechanism: Spring
Height: 2"
Value Index: 3

Description: Church bell
Material: Lead
Origin: Unknown
Mechanism: Wind-up
Height: 1.5"
Value Index: 5

Description: Bell
Material: Vegetable ivory
Origin: Unknown
Mechanism: Wind-up
Height: 2"
Value Index: 2

Description: Dinner bell
Material: Brass
Origin: Unknown
Mechanism: Wind-up
Height: 2.5"
Value Index: 4

Description: Bell,"From THE DOUGLAS
 ROOM, STIRLING CASTLE"
Material: Wood (Tartanware)
Origin: Unknown
Mechanism: Wind-up
Height: 2.25"
Value Index: 3

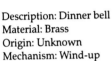

Left
Description: Bell
Material: Wood
Origin: Unknown
Mechanism: Wind-up
Height: 1.75"
Value Index: 3

Right
Description: Bell
Material: Wood (Mauchline)
Origin: Unknown
Mechanism: Wind-up
Height: 2.5"
Value Index: 3

124

Description: Upright piano
Material: Brass, celluloid
Origin: Unknown
Mechanism: Spring
Height: 2.5"
Value Index: 4

Description: Baby grand piano
Material: Metal
Origin: Germany
Mechanism: Spring
Height: 1.5"
Value Index: 4

Left
Description: Mandolin
Material: Celluloid, tortoiseshell
Origin: Unknown
Mechanism: Spring
Height: 1.25" (4.5" length)
Value Index: 3

Right
Description: Mandolin
Material: Celluloid
Origin: Unknown
Mechanism: Spring
Height: 1" (3.75" length)
Value Index: 4

Description: Mandolin (two variations)
Material: Enamelled brass (left), brass (right)
Origin: Unknown
Mechanism: Wind-up
Height: 2.75"
Value Index: 4

Below
Description: Double bass
Material: Celluloid
Origin: Unknown
Mechanism: Spring
Height: 1" (5.25" length)
Value Index: 4

Above
Description: Cello with bow
Material: Brass
Origin: Unknown
Mechanism: Wind-up
Height: 2.5"
Value Index: 4

Description: Punch and Judy music box, plays
    music when wound
Material: Brass
Origin: Unknown
Mechanism: Wind-up
Height: 1.5"
Value Index: 5

126

Description: Drum with scenes (two variations)
Material: Brass, celluloid
Origin: Unknown
Mechanism: Spring
Height: 2"
Value Index: 3

Description: Drum with scenes (reverse of pre-
    vious photograph)
Material: Brass, celluloid
Origin: Unknown
Mechanism: Spring
Height: 2"
Value Index: 3

Description: Drum with sticks (two color variations)
Material: Brass, celluloid
Origin: Unknown
Mechanism: Wind-up
Height: 1" (2" diameter)
Value Index: 3

Description: American Civil War drum with sticks
Material: Brass, celluloid
Origin: Unknown
Mechanism: Spring
Height: 1.5"
Value Index: 4

Description: Pipe organ, plays music when wound
Material: Brass
Origin: Unknown
Mechanism: Wind-up
Height: 1.5"
Value Index: 5

Chapter 9
Clocks

Clocks are the most common single object represented in the tape measures. The great variety includes carriage, alarm and mantle clocks. Some have hands that turn as the tape is pulled. Others incorporate additional features such as stanhopes, which were miniature "peepholes" showing scenes of famous castles or tourist sights. Clocks are the most common tape measures made of bakelite, although celluloid and metal examples are also found.

Description: Triangular carriage clock (three color variations)
Material: Brass, celluloid
Origin: Germany
Mechanism: Spring
Height: 1.5"
Value Index: 3

Description: Three-legged alarm clock (three color variations)
Material: Metal
Origin: Germany
Mechanism: Wind-up
Height: 1.75"
Value Index: 2

Left
Description: Round clock face
Material: Metal
Origin: Germany
Mechanism: Spring
Height: 1.5"
Value Index: 2

Center
Description: Pocket watch
Material: Brass
Origin: Germany
Mechanism: Spring
Height: 2"
Value Index: 3

Right
Description: Alarm clock
Material: Metal
Origin: Japan
Mechanism: Spring
Height: 1.5"
Value Index: 2

Above left
Description: Square carriage clock
Material: Brass, celluloid
Origin: Germany
Mechanism: Spring
Height: 1.75"
Value Index: 2

Description: Fancy clock
Material: Brass
Origin: Unknown
Mechanism: Wind-up
Height: 2"
Value Index: 3

Above right
Description: Square clock
Material: Brass
Origin: Unknown
Mechanism: Wind-up
Height: 2"
Value Index: 2

Description: Three-legged
    clock with stanhope
Material: Celluloid
Origin: Unknown
Mechanism: Wind-up
Height: 2.25"
Value Index: 5

130

Above left
Description: Rectangular mantle clock
Material: Bakelite
Origin: Germany
Mechanism: Spring
Height: 2"
Value Index: 2

Above center
Description: Curved mantle clock
Material: Bakelite
Origin: Germany
Mechanism: Spring
Height: 2.25"
Value Index: 2

Above right
Description: Arched mantle clock
Material: Bakelite
Origin: Germany
Mechanism: Spring
Height: 1.5"
Value Index: 2

Left
Description: Mantle clock
Material: Celluloid
Origin: Unknown
Mechanism: Spring
Height: 1.5"
Value Index: 3

Right
Description: Mantle clock
Material: Celluloid
Origin: Germany
Mechanism: Spring
Height: 2"
Value Index: 3

Description: Clock with columns
Material: Celluloid
Origin: Germany
Mechanism: Spring
Height: 2.25"
Value Index: 4

131

Chapter 10
Clothing and
accessories

Hats and footwear are common subjects for tape measures. Hats come in all shapes, from flat-brimmed Derbys to tall top hats. A variety of footwear styles includes rough hiking boots and fancy ladies' shoes with decorative stones or pearls.

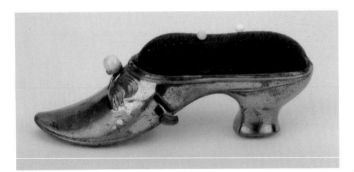

Description: Shoe with pearl
Material: Brass
Origin: Unknown
Mechanism: Wind-up
Height: 1"
Value Index: 3

Description: Moccasin
Material: Leather, beads
Origin: Japan
Mechanism: Spring
Height: 1.25"
Value Index: 2

Description: Shoe (also pincushion)
Material: Rubber
Origin: Japan
Mechanism: Spring
Height: 1.75"
Value Index: 1

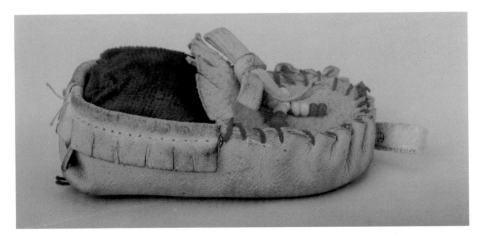

Left
Description: Roller skate (also pincushion)
Material: Brass
Origin: Unknown
Mechanism: Wind-up
Height: 1.75"
Value Index: 5

Right
Description: Roller skate
Material: Celluloid
Origin: Unknown
Mechanism: Spring
Height: 1.75"
Value Index: 3

Left
Description: Hiking boot with crystal and cane
Material: Brass
Origin: Unknown
Mechanism: Wind-up
Height: 1.5"
Value Index: 3

Center left
Description: Hiking boot
Material: Brass
Origin: English
Mechanism: Wind-up
Height: 1.5"
Value Index: 3

Center right
Description: Boot with buffalo
Material: Brass
Origin: Unknown
Mechanism: Wind-up
Height: 2"
Value Index: 3

Right
Description: Hiking boot with cane
Material: Brass
Origin: Unknown
Mechanism: Wind-up
Height: 1.5"
Value Index: 3

Left
Description: Royal crown
Material: Brass, velvet
Origin: Unknown
Mechanism: Spring
Height: 2"
Value Index: 4

Right
Description: Crown
Material: Celluloid
Origin: Unknown
Mechanism: Spring
Height: 1.5"
Value Index: 3

Left
Description: German helmet
Material: Metal, brass
Origin: Unknown
Mechanism: Wind-up
Height: 1.75"
Value Index: 5

Right
Description: German helmet
Material: Metal, brass
Origin: Unknown
Mechanism: Wind-up
Height: 1.75"
Value Index: 5

Description: Flat hat
Material: Celluloid
Origin: Unknown
Mechanism: Spring
Height: 0.75"
Value Index: 3

134

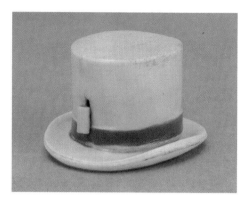

Description: Canteen with food plate
Material: Celluloid
Origin: Unknown
Mechanism: Spring
Height: 2.25"
Value Index: 3

Description: Top hat
Material: Celluloid
Origin: Unknown
Mechanism: Spring
Height: 1.25"
Value Index: 3

Description: Fedora
Material: Celluloid
Origin: Unknown
Mechanism: Spring
Height: 0.75"
Value Index: 3

Below left and center
Description: Purse (two color variations)
Material: Celluloid
Origin: Germany
Mechanism: Spring
Height: 1.75"
Value Index: 3

Below right
Description: Purse
Material: Celluloid
Origin: Unknown
Mechanism: Spring
Height: 2"
Value Index: 3

Description: Backpack
Material: Celluloid
Origin: Japan
Mechanism: Spring
Height: 2.5" x 1.25"
Value Index: 2

Chapter 11
Household items

The tape measures in this category give a real "feel" for everyday life. From Victorian spinning wheels and copper coffee grinders to wall telephones and hand mirrors, this group encompasses a wide range of historical artifacts.

Description: Ewer
Material: Brass
Origin: Unknown
Mechanism: Wind-up
Height: 1.75"
Value Index: 4

Description: Saucepan
Material: Copper
Origin: Unknown
Mechanism: Wind-up
Height: 1.25"
Value Index: 4

Description: Spinning wheel (pincushion)
Material: Metal
Origin: Unknown
Mechanism: Wind-up
Height: 5"
Value Index: 5

Description: Samovar
Material: Brass, white metal
Origin: Unknown
Mechanism: Wind-up
Height: 2.25"
Value Index: 5

Left
Description: Elegant coffee pot
Material: Brass
Origin: Unknown
Mechanism: Wind-up
Height: 2"
Value Index: 3

Right
Description: Coffee pot
Material: Metal, bone knob
Origin: Unknown
Mechanism: Wind-up
Height: 1.75"
Value Index: 4

Left
Description: Tea kettle with stand
Material: White metal
Origin: Unknown
Mechanism: Wind-up
Height: 2"
Value Index: 3

Right
Description: Tea kettle with stand
Material: White metal, agate handle
Origin: Unknown
Mechanism: Wind-up
Height: 2.25"
Value Index: 4

Description: Tea kettle with scalloped handle
Material: Brass
Origin: Unknown
Mechanism: Wind-up
Height: 2"
Value Index: 4

Left
Description: Coffee pot
Material: White metal, brass
Origin: "London Made Austria"
Mechanism: Wind-up
Height: 1.75"
Value Index: 3

Right
Description: Coffee pot
Material: Brass
Origin: "London Made Austria"
Mechanism: Wind-up
Height: 1.5"
Value Index: 5

Description: Stein
Material: Brass
Origin: "London Made In Austria"
Mechanism: Wind-up
Height: 1.5"
Value Index: 4

Left
Description: Chocolate pot
Material: Brass, agate handle
Origin: Unknown
Mechanism: Wind-up
Height: 2.25"
Value Index: 4

Right
Description: Chocolate pot
Material: White metal, agate handle
Origin: Unknown
Mechanism: Wind-up
Height: 2.25"
Value Index: 4

Description: Cup and saucer with spoon
Material: Brass
Origin: Unknown
Mechanism: Wind-up
Height: 1.5"
Value Index: 4

Description: Punch bowl with ladle
Material: Brass
Origin: Unknown
Mechanism: Wind-up
Height: 1.25"
Value Index: 4

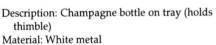

Description: Champagne bottle on tray (holds
    thimble)
Material: White metal
Origin: Unknown
Mechanism: Wind-up
Height: 2.25"
Value Index: 4

Left
Description: Champagne bottle in iced cooler
Material: Brass, celluloid
Origin: Germany
Mechanism: Wind-up
Height: 2.25"
Value Index: 4

Right
Description: Champagne bottle in cooler
Material: Brass
Origin: Unknown
Mechanism: Wind-up
Height: 2.5"
Value Index: 3

Description: Flask
Material: Celluloid
Origin: Germany
Mechanism: Spring
Height: 2"
Value Index: 3

Left
Description: Whiskey bottle (Calvert)
Material: Bakelite
Origin: Unknown
Mechanism: Spring
Height: 3.25"
Value Index: 2

Right
Description: Wine bottle (Veuve Cliquot)
Material: Metal, brass
Origin: Unknown
Mechanism: Wind-up
Height: 2"
Value Index: 2

Description: Coffee grinder
Material: Copper
Origin: Unknown
Mechanism: Wind-up
Height: 1.5"
Value Index: 3

Description: Mixer/grater
Material: Wood
Origin: Unknown
Mechanism: Wind-up
Height: 2.5"
Value Index: 2

Description: Butter churn
Material: Wood
Origin: Unknown
Mechanism: Wind-up
Height: 2.5"
Value Index: 2

Left
Description: Coffee grinder
Material: Celluloid, brass
Origin: Unknown
Mechanism: Spring
Height: 1.5"
Value Index: 3

Right
Description: Coffee grinder
Material: Brass
Origin: Germany
Mechanism: Wind-up
Height: 1.75"
Value Index: 3

Left
Description: Coffee grinder
Material: Mauchline
Origin: Unknown
Mechanism: Wind-up
Height: 2.5"
Value Index: 3

Right
Description: Churn
Material: Mauchline
Origin: Unknown
Mechanism: Wind-up
Height: 2.25"
Value Index: 3

Description: Water tub with mirror
Material: Celluloid
Origin: Unknown
Mechanism: Spring
Height: 1.25"
Value Index: 3

Description: Nutmeg grater
Material: White metal
Origin: Unknown
Mechanism: Wind-up
Height: 1"
Value Index: 4

Description: Stein
Material: Celluloid
Origin: Unknown
Mechanism: Spring
Height: 2"
Value Index: 3

Description: Sadiron
Material: Brass, agate
Origin: Unknown
Mechanism: Wind-up
Height: 2"
Value Index: 3

Left
Description: Bucket
Material: Celluloid
Origin: Unknown
Mechanism: Spring
Height: 2.25"
Value Index: 3

Right
Description: Cream pail
Material: Brass
Origin: Austria
Mechanism: Wind-up
Height: 1.5"
Value Index: 4

Description: Watering can (also pincushion)
Material: Brass
Origin: Unknown
Mechanism: Wind-up
Height: 2"
Value Index: 4

Below left
Description: Lamp on stand
Material: Brass, celluloid
Origin: Germany
Mechanism: Spring
Height: 2.25"
Value Index: 3

Below right
Description: Lamp on stand
Material: Brass, celluloid
Origin: Germany
Mechanism: Spring
Height: 2.5"
Value Index: 3

Description: Lamp on stand
Material: Brass, celluloid
Origin: Germany
Mechanism: Spring
Height: 2.25"
Value Index: 3

Description: Lawn roller
Material: Brass, felt
Origin: Unknown
Mechanism: Wind-up
Height: 4"
Value Index: 4

143

Description: Victorian style lamp
Material: Celluloid
Origin: Germany
Mechanism: Spring
Height: 2"
Value Index: 3

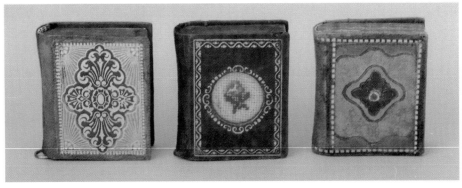

Above–Description: Book (three color variations)
    Material: Leather
    Origin: Unknown
    Mechanism: Spring
    Height: 2"
    Value Index: 2

Below–Description: Book (three color variations)
    Material: Celluloid
    Origin: Unknown
    Mechanism: Spring
    Height: 2"
    Value Index: 2

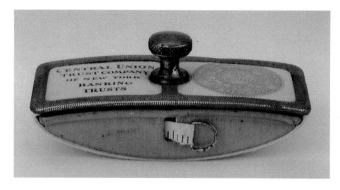

Description: Ink blotter
Material: Brass, celluloid
Origin: Germany
Mechanism: Spring
Height: 1.5"
Value Index: 2

Description: Spool of thread
Material: Brass
Origin: Unknown
Mechanism: Wind-up
Height: 1.25"
Value Index: 4

Description: Wall telephone
Material: White metal
Origin: Germany
Mechanism: Wind-up
Height: 2.75"
Value Index: 5

Description: Napkin ring
Material: Brass
Origin: Unknown
Mechanism: Wind-up
Height: 1.5"
Value Index: 4

Description: Thimble
Material: Celluloid
Origin: Unknown
Mechanism: Spring
Height: 1.25"
Value Index: 3

Description: Pin tree
Material: Brass, celluloid
Origin: Germany
Mechanism: Spring
Height: 2.5"
Value Index: 3

Description: Basket (also pincushion)
Material: Celluloid
Origin: Unknown
Mechanism: Spring
Height: 1.25"
Value Index: 2

Description: Sewing machine
Material: Metal, tortoiseshell
Origin: Germany
Mechanism: Wind-up
Height: 2.25"
Value Index: R

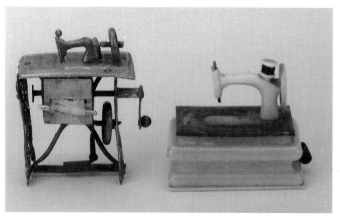

Above left
Description: Sewing machine
Material: Brass
Origin: Unknown
Mechanism: Wind-up
Height: 2"
Value Index: 5

Above right
Description: Sewing machine
Material: Celluloid, tortoiseshell
Origin: Unknown
Mechanism: Spring
Height: 1.75"
Value Index: 4

Right
Description: Hand mirror
Material: Stippled celluloid
Origin: Germany
Mechanism: Spring
Height: 3.5"
Rarity: 4

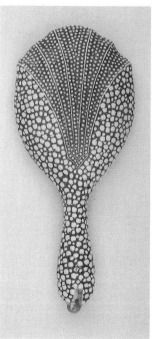

Description: Bellows
Material: Celluloid
Origin: Unknown
Mechanism: Spring
Height: 2.5"
Rarity: 4

Description: Lock
Material: Celluloid
Origin: Unknown
Mechanism: Spring
Height: 1.75"
Value Index: 3

Description: Dress box
Material: Celluloid
Origin: Unknown
Mechanism: Spring
Height: 1.75"
Value Index: 3

Left
Description: Round Hoover vacuum cleaner
Material: Celluloid
Origin: Unknown
Mechanism: Spring
Height: 1.75"
Value Index: 1

Right
Description: Hoover upright
Material: Plastic
Origin: USA
Mechanism: Spring
Height: 5.25"
Value Index: 1

148

Chapter 12
Miscellaneous
items

Many of the most unusual tape measures do not fall into any of the previous categories. From carousels to billiard tables and roller skates, these are some of the most ingenious and sought after tape measures. One subgroup, the Disney characters, are particularly rare and valuable.

Description: Donald Duck
Material: Celluloid
Origin: Japan
Mechanism: Spring
Height: 2.75"
Rarity: R

Description: Snow White (also pincushion)
Material: Celluloid
Origin: Unknown
Mechanism: Spring
Height: 3"
Rarity: R

Description: Goofy
Material: Celluloid
Origin: Japan
Mechanism: Spring
Height: 2.25"
Rarity: R

Left
Description: Minnie Mouse
Material: Celluloid
Origin: Japan
Mechanism: Spring
Height: 2.25"
Rarity: R

Right
Description: Mickey Mouse
Material: Celluloid
Origin: Japan
Mechanism: Spring
Height: 2.25"
Rarity: R

Description: Billiards table
Material: Celluloid
Origin: Unknown
Mechanism: Spring
Height: 1.5"
Value Index: 4

Description: Game table, "No. 169 Collection of President and Mrs. Franklin Delano Roosevelt"
Material: Celluloid
Origin: Unknown
Mechanism: Spring
Height: 1.75"
Value Index: 5

Description: Baby cradle (also pincushion)
Material: Brass
Origin: Unknown
Mechanism: Wind-up
Height: 1.5"
Value Index: 5

Description: Table (also pincushion)
Material: Brass
Origin: Unknown
Mechanism: Spring
Height: 2"
Value Index: 3

Description: Binoculars
Material: Metal
Origin: Unknown
Mechanism: Wind-up
Height: 1.75"
Rarity: 5

Description: Box camera
Material: Celluloid
Origin: Unknown
Mechanism: Wind-up
Height: 1.5"
Rarity: 5

Description: Sun face
Material: Celluloid
Origin: Unknown
Mechanism: Spring
Height: 1.5"
Rarity: 3

Description: Wheelbarrow with rabbit
Material: Brass, felt
Origin: Unknown
Mechanism: Wind-up
Height: 2.75"
Rarity: 5

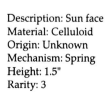

151

Description: Snowman
Material: Celluloid
Origin: Unknown
Mechanism: Spring
Height: 1"
Rarity: 3

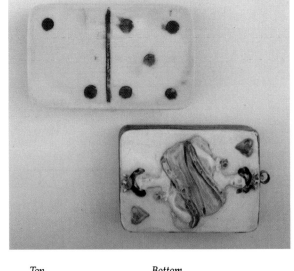

Description: Nest with three eggs
Material: Celluloid
Origin: Germany
Mechanism: Spring
Height: 0.75" (1.25" diameter)
Rarity: 4

Top
Description: Domino
Material: Celluloid
Origin: Unknown
Mechanism: Spring
Height: 2"
Rarity: 3

Bottom
Description: Queen of hearts
Material: Celluloid
Origin: Germany
Mechanism: Spring
Height: 1.5"
Rarity: 2

Description: Chariot (two color variations)
Material: Celluloid
Origin: Germany
Mechanism: Spring
Height: 2"
Value Index: 3

Description: Bridge die
Material: Celluloid
Origin: Unknown
Mechanism: Spring
Height: 1"
Rarity: 3

Description: Dice shaker
Material: Brass
Origin: Unknown
Mechanism: Wind-up
Height: 1"
Rarity: 3

Description: Cash register (two types of metal)
Material: Brass (left), white metal (right)
Origin: Unknown
Mechanism: Wind-up
Height: 2"
Rarity: 3

Description: Book press
Material: Brass
Origin: Unknown
Mechanism: Wind-up
Height: 2"
Rarity: 4

Description: Carousel
Material: Brass
Origin: Unknown
Mechanism: Wind-up
Height: 2.75"
Rarity: R

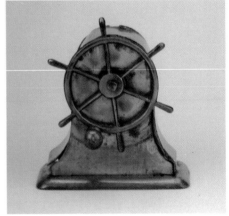

Description: Children's game
Material: Brass
Origin: Unknown
Mechanism: Wind-up
Height: 2"
Rarity: 5

Description: Ship's wheel
Material: Copper
Origin: English
Mechanism: Wind-up
Height: 1.5"
Rarity: 3

Description: Wheel
Material: Brass
Origin: Unknown
Mechanism: Wind-up
Height: 2"
Rarity: 3

Description: Golden Rule
Material: Brass
Origin: Unknown
Mechanism: Spring
Height: 1"
Value Index: 2

Left
Description: Dress form
Material: Bakelite
Origin: Unknown
Mechanism: Spring
Height: 4"
Rarity: 2

Right
Description: Dress form
Material: White metal
Origin: Unknown
Mechanism: Spring
Height: 3"
Rarity: 2

Left
Description: Clam shell, "A Clam with Three
    Feet"
Material: Sterling
Origin: Unknown
Mechanism: Spring
Height: 2.25"
Rarity: 3

Right
Description: Clam shell
Material: White metal
Origin: Unknown
Mechanism: Spring
Height: 2.25"
Rarity: 3

155

Description: Scale
Material: Metal
Origin: Unknown
Mechanism: Wind-up
Height: 1.75"
Rarity: 3

Top left
Description: Turtle, "Pull My Head Not My Leg"
Material: Metal
Origin: Unknown
Mechanism: Spring
Height: 0.5" (2.25" length)
Value Index: 3

Top right
Description: Flask, "I Made Kentuckey Famous in a Measure"
Material: Brass
Origin: Unknown
Mechanism: Spring
Height: 2"
Value Index: 3

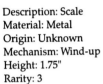

Description: Globe
Material: Gold-colored metal
Origin: Japan
Mechanism: Spring
Height: 1.25"
Rarity: 1

Bottom left
Description: Hat, "Most Hats Cover the Head, I Cover the Feet"
Material: Brass
Origin: Unknown
Mechanism: Spring
Height: 1.5"
Value Index: 3

Bottom right
Description: Shoe, "Three Feet in One Shoe"
Material: Brass
Origin: Unknown
Mechanism: Spring
Height: 1.5"
Value Index: 3

Description: Golf ball with clubs
Material: Brass
Origin: Unknown
Mechanism: Wind-up
Height: 1"
Rarity: 4

Description: Bread roll (?)
Material: Celluloid
Origin: "London Made Austria"
Mechanism: Wind-up
Height: 0.75"
Value Index: 3

Description: Globe
Material: Metal
Origin: Unknown
Mechanism: Spring
Height: 2"
Rarity: 2

Left
Description: Periwinkle (pincushion)
Material: Shell
Origin: Unknown
Mechanism: Wind-up
Height: 2"
Rarity: 5

Right
Description: Cowrie shell
Material: Shell
Origin: Unknown
Mechanism: Wind-up
Height: 1.5"
Rarity: 5

Description: Golf ball
Material: Celluloid
Origin: Germany
Mechanism: Spring
Height: 1.75"
Rarity: 3

Description: Barrel
Material: Celluloid
Origin: Great Britain
Mechanism: Spring
Height: 1.75"
Rarity: 2

Description: Barrel with stanhope (three vari-
    eties)
Material: Vegetable ivory, bone
Origin: Unknown
Mechanism: Wind-up
Height: 1.75"
Rarity: 2

Description: Tapes from the 1940s and 1950s (se-
    lection)
Material: Ceramic, plastic
Origin: Unknown
Mechanism: Spring
Height: varies 2"-4"
Rarity: 1

Description: Barrel
Material: Celluloid
Origin: Unknown
Mechanism: Wind-up
Height: 2"
Rarity: 2

Above left
Description: Tower (pincushion)
Material: Ivory
Origin: Unknown
Mechanism: Wind-up
Height: 3"
Rarity: 4

Above center
Description: Castle
Material: Vegetable ivory, bone
Origin: Unknown
Mechanism: Wind-up
Height: 1.5"
Rarity: 4

Above right
Description: Tower (also pincushion)
Material: Vegetable ivory, bone
Origin: Unknown
Mechanism: Wind-up
Height: 3.25"
Rarity: 4

Below left
Description: Acorn with stanhope
Material: Vegetable ivory, bone
Origin: Unknown
Mechanism: Wind-up
Height: 1.75"
Rarity: 2

Below right
Description: Tower
Material: Vegetable ivory, bone
Origin: Unknown
Mechanism: Wind-up
Height: 2"
Rarity: 2

Bibliography

Groves, Sylvia. *The History of Needlework Tools and Accessories*. Newton Abbot: David and Charles, 1973.

Horowitz, Estelle. "Measurement and Tape Measures." *Needle Arts* (Winter, 1983), pp. 2-3.

Hurt, Zuelia Ann. "Craft Tools--Then and Now." *Decorating and Craft Ideas* (November, 1981), p. 30.

Jary, Linda Gordanier. "Ells and Yards, Nails and Inches." *Sampler of Antique Needlework Quarterly* (Vol. 9), pp. 20-25.

Rogers, Gay Ann. *An Illustrated History of Needlework Tools*. London: John Murray, 1983.

Whiting, Gertrude. *Old-Time Tools and Toys of Needlework*. New York: Dover Publications, 1971.

Zalkin, Estelle. *Thimbles and Sewing Implements*. Willow Grove: Warman Publishing Co., 1988.

Description: Tapes from the 1940s and 1950s (selection)
Material: Fabric
Origin: Unknown

Mechanism: Spring
Height: varies 2"-5"
Rarity: 1